WHEN YOU'VE MADE IT YOUR OWN . . .

WHEN YOU'VE MADE IT YOUR OWN...

Teaching Poetry to Young People

GREGORY A. DENMAN

With a Foreword by Bill Martin Jr

Heinemann
Portsmouth, NH

HEINEMANN EDUCATIONAL BOOKS, INC.
361 Hanover Street   Portsmouth, NH   03801-3959
Offices and agents throughout the world

The following have generously given permission to use quotations from copyrighted works:

Prologue: "Stopping by Woods" from *The Poetry of Robert Frost* edited by Edward Connery
Lathem. Copyright © 1969 by Holt, Rinehart and Winston, Inc. Copyright © 1962 by Robert
Frost. Copyright © 1975 by Lesley Frost Ballantine. Reprinted by permission of Henry Holt and
Company, Inc.

Introduction: "The Road Not Taken" from *The Poetry of Robert Frost* edited by Edward Connery
Lathem. Copyright © 1969 by Holt, Rinehart and Winston, Inc. Copyright © 1962 by Robert
Frost. Copyright © 1975 by Lesley Frost Ballantine. Reprinted by permission of Henry Holt and
Company, Inc.

Chapter 1: From "i thank You God for most this amazing." Copyright 1947 by E. E. Cummings;
renewed 1975 by Nancy T. Andrews. Reprinted from "i thank You God for most this amazing"
Complete Poems 1913–1962 by E. E. Cummings by permission of Harcourt Brace Jovanovich,
Inc.

(*Acknowledgments continue on page* 197.)

Library of Congress Cataloging-in-Publication Data
   Denman, Gregory.
      When you've made it your own— : teaching poetry to young people /
   by Gregory Denman ; with a foreword by Bill Martin, Jr.
         p. cm.
      Bibliography: p.
      Includes index.
      ISBN 0–435–08462–3
      1. Poetry—Study and teaching (Elementary)   I. Title.
   PN1101.D46 1988
   372.6′4—dc19   88–2989
                                                                        CIP

Figures by Michael E. Cellan and Wladislaw Finne.
Designed by Wladislaw Finne.
Printed in the United States of America.
10 9 8 7 6   5   4

Dedicated,
respectfully,
to
Bill Martin Jr:
friend
and
mentor

CONTENTS

FOREWORD

The important thing about Gregory Denman is that he's a master teacher. He's a poet and he's a "poem-teller." He's an actor and he's a "rainmaker." He's a lecturer and he's a "circuit rider." But the important thing about Gregory Denman is that he's a master teacher.

Once you've encountered this messenger, this "Johnny Poem-seeder," you'll never be the same. He expands your imagination, stirs you up, sets you thinking and dreaming and daring and doing. And you start circumnavigating right brain/left brain/from up to down and twice around—trying to catch the will-o-the-wisp in sounds that are much more felt than heard.

If this seems gamesy and playful, just accept that it is. He means it that way. He is out to snare you, to stay you, with moments of wonder that expand the size and clarity of the world we live in, with threaded adventures that lead to opening glimpses of truth and beauty. It's all flittingly romantic, but it's hands-on-the-plow too. You dance on his lightning rod like a spark of electricity. At the same time, you respond directly and meaningfully, with childlike confidence, to his thesis.

Kids learn best about language and how it works by absorbing poetry by the yard, he believes, by imprinting poems in memory with the immediacy of pressing the hand into wet clay. The imprint carries the message. If this be true, and I think it is, then a delighting poem can push any day, every day, in the right direction.

That's what this book is about. It's a snowballing statement of a teacher who believes that what he does and doesn't do can make a difference in children's ability to survive an increasingly complex and uncaring world. This author, this poet, this playground professor, lays himself on the line, not because he has to, but because he cares. It's a distinguished choice.

Bill Martin Jr

PROLOGUE

When you've made it your own . . .

The day was right. The trees in the park across from school had shed their fall coats and in their bareness revealed their innermost shapes, the movement and direction of their branches, the upward thrust of their trunks. An overcast sky created a solemn quietness with the gray.

All right, gang, grab your art boards and paper . . .
we're going to the park for Language.

Their faces perked up, delighting in the incongruity of Language with art materials, but they said nothing. I could almost hear them thinking, "We'll see what he's up to today." We headed out in the archetype of an elementary school's single-file-quiet-in-the-halls procession. I stuck my head in the office door as we passed and said,

Fifth grade's going to the park for Language.
Be back in an hour or so.

My principal nodded with that same queer look he gave me whenever I did such things. His expression seemed to question quietly the value of teachers' tenure.

Once at the park we sat down and began to notice the trees.

Look as carefully as you can at the whole shapes of the trees.
Follow one from the base up through all the branches,
over the top and down the other side to the ground.

Imagine that your eye is your pencil tracing the entire outline of
the tree.

Find a favorite branch and put your arm into its shape.
See where other branches overlap your branch.

What shapes are outlined by the crossing of the branches?

Draw the shape of the tree with your fingers in the air.

When you're ready, guide your pencils around the shapes of the trees on your papers.

"Hey, Mr. D., I thought this was supposed to be Language," blurts out my ever-present "supposed-to-be" monitor.

'Tis, my friend, 'tis.

Soon, marvelously detailed shapes of bare trees begin appearing on the papers. Outlined branches are overlapping and extending over the edges of some. The base of the trunks forms the contour of the ground.

We snake back through the halls, past the office.

Time for art, I grin.

Back in the room I discuss key art terms: contour lines (the outlining of an object), negative space (the background of any drawing or painting in which there are no objects), and perspective (trees close appearing larger; those farther away, smaller).

Now I say, "Look at your picture. I want you to imagine that you are deep in the woods, miles from anywhere, in the middle of winter. It's pitch black out." They sit and look at their work and the scene. "How can we create what you're imagining on paper?" I ask.

They respond, "We can color all the negative space black and leave the ground pure white." The image has fixed. They begin carefully to paint with Magic Markers and India ink. The spell is cast and I begin. Walking around the room as they paint, looking over their shoulders, I talk as if to myself:

Whose woods these are I think I know.
His house is in the village though;
He will not see me stopping here
To watch his woods fill up with snow.

They continue what they're doing, not really noticing me, but hearing.

My little horse must think it queer
To stop without a farmhouse near
Between the woods and frozen lake
The darkest evening of the year.

Their painting strokes have found the same rhythm as my voice.

He gives his harness bells a shake
To ask if there is some mistake.
The only other sound's the sweep
Of easy wind and downy flake.

Occasionally they look up with that "strange—Mr. Denman" look.
I smile. I'm very comfortable.

The woods are lovely, dark and deep,
But I have promises to keep,
And miles to go before I sleep.
And miles to go before I sleep.

For a good bit of the morning I continue, reciting the poem over
and over. At times they join in with lines. I write the poem's words
on the board. Looking at their art and the words, they immediately
see. "Hey, that's the poem that goes with my picture." I tell them
all about Robert Frost and my impressions of the poem and draw
their impressions from them.

I show them illustrated volumes of Frost's books. We discuss
whether professional illustrators had the same images in their minds
as the students did while they were drawing and listening. "Which
image is correct?" I ask them. "Is there a correct image?"

We talk about the poem, particularly its last lines.

What promises do you think he had?
What promises do you have? Can you share them?

When my teacher instinct tells me that we have gone as far as
we should, I tell them, "Listen, my friends, when *you've* made the
poem *your* own, come back and share it with us."

In a few days half the class has the poem completely memorized,
and they recite with a moving sense of understanding. Others have
returned with the words integrated in the snow of their art work.
Some relate having talked about the poem with their parents and
how—wonder of wonders—their parents not only knew of the poem
but still could recite a line or two. Some still need time for the poem
to become their own. That's okay, too.

By the end of the week the room is cluttered with art work, we
can chorus the poem together, and a bit of poetry has become our
own.

INTRODUCTION

A few years ago, while I was still teaching in an elementary school, I happened to be in our teachers' lounge one lunch period when the conversation turned to a project of one of the teachers in the building. This teacher, who was completing a master's degree at a local college, had come to know one of her professors quite well and was having a poem she had recently "discovered" written out in calligraphy as a small gift for him. The professor, I gathered from the conversation, was at a crossroads in his career and was thinking about doing something different with his life for a while. The teacher was passing the poem around. No one seemed to recognize it. Upon seeing me and knowing my love of poetry, she asked if I had ever read it. She handed me the poem, and I read the first line:

Two roads diverged in a yellow wood,

I stopped and, trying to mask my utter surprise, looked around the room and asked if anyone had read or head this poem before. No one had!

I remember thinking to myself, "My God, here is a group of talented and dedicated elementary teachers, some with master's degrees, and they've never heard of Robert Frost's 'The Road Not Taken.' " I found it hard to believe that anyone at all, much less a group of teachers, could get through our educational system and have missed that well-known poem. Besides being a most moving and beautifully simple poem, it is as much a part of the American literate culture as the Great Plains of the Midwest and the Rocky Mountains are a part of the American landscape.

I assumed everyone was familiar with Robert Frost.

Why, my fifth graders that year had heard me recite and talk about not only "The Road Not Taken," but "Birches" as well. With India ink they had drawn and painted beautiful black-on-white scenes to illustrate "Stopping by Woods on a Snowy Evening." In addition to Frost we had read and talked about many of Carl Sandburg's poems; had a sad moment with Edna St. Vincent Millay's "The Ballad of the Harp Weaver"; rolled with laughter and delight during many readings of some of the Yukon tales of Robert Service; and been absolutely enchanted by "The Mountain Whippoorwill" by Stephen Vincent Benét. We modeled much of what we wrote on some of the finest American poets. We held assemblies during the year in which my class would recite poem after poem with the emotion and understanding of first-year acting students.

But my class, I later discovered, was an exception. I was simply, for better or for worse, an individual teacher who happened to love poetry personally and was able to teach it successfully. Poetry had naturally tied into my writing program, complemented my science and social studies, and was a basic part of most of my reading lessons.

If a poem such as "The Road Not Taken" was unfamiliar to these teachers, what poetry was being taught? Or, more importantly, *was* any being taught? At the time of the occurrence with the poem in the teachers' lounge, I maintained a side career as a professional storyteller. Using summers and professional time allowed by my school district, I visited schools as a storyteller, and my programs naturally included many poems. In 1984 this sideline blossomed into the beginnings of a career as a full-time storyteller and language arts consultant, and now, in addition to teaching university classes, I travel to many schools each year and talk to literally thousands of teachers and many thousands of students. I have discovered that the unfamiliarity with American poetry I noticed in my school is not unique. In many schools, poetry beyond a very primary type of jingle or poem is an unfamiliar beast. A hobgoblin of sorts. A monster to teach.

While I visit schools I've made it a habit to chat with teachers about their poetry instruction. Many, like me, have a deep love and understanding of poetry. Many others, however, confess to never having taken a beginning poetry class and are quite understandably frustrated by poetry. Somehow good teachers are getting certified without any substantial work in poetry, and their classes in turn get a meager portion of the subject.

Through my observations I have identified some common problems in the poetry instruction in our elementary schools:

• *Poetry does not endure in today's curriculum.* After the peppy, enthusiastic, primary years when kids love jingles and rhymes and the very simple poems included in their basals, their interest in poetry declines. It becomes difficult to teach and is de-emphasized in the curriculum.

- *Poetry is inappropriately taught.* Poetry is either sidelined as a not-all-that-important extra or lumped in with the same teaching mode as reading: vocabulary, silent reading, oral reading, and comprehension questions. Or, in the later grades, poetry becomes solely that dreaded two-week language arts unit, rarely mentioned prior to or after the unit.
- *Familiarity with traditional American poetry is not stressed as an essential part of an American child's education.* The most common poetic forms taught appear to be the haiku and limerick, neither of which is particularly American. The whole field of truly American poetry is not aggressively taught in our schools.
- *Teachers' use of non-basal resources in poetry instruction is limited.* The most widely used non-basal textbook is Kenneth Koch's *Wishes, Lies and Dreams*—a very fine book, I might say, but quite repetitive if used exclusively. After visiting an elementary school and its adjacent middle school in one area, I estimated that a given child moving through that system might have seven years of "I used to be a tadpole, but now I am a frog."
- *Poems taught to children are justified more by their popularity with the kids than their value in helping children become, eventually, mature readers of poetry.* By far the most popular poetry books are, of course, Shel Silverstein's *Where the Sidewalk Ends* and *The Light in the Attic.* The books are simply wonderful, but they hardly have to be taught: Put them in the hands of children and they teach themselves. There is, however, much more poetry, admittedly not as immediately popular, of which I feel children need to become aware.

My responses to these problems and deficiencies are the basis of this book. A good part of my work now, when I'm not teaching or telling stories, is conducting workshops on poetry. Much of what I demonstrate in my workshops is aimed at helping teachers become more comfortable with their teaching of poetry and, I hope, their students, more aware of the magic of poetry. I like to think that I help good language arts teachers become even better poetry teachers. And since at least half of my workshop has always been devoted to my performance of poetry, I hope that the teachers themselves become wonderfully entangled in the poet's magic word web.

This book is not meant to be a teacher's manual, although I've included many activities that can be done in classes. Nor is this book to be seen an adequate substitute for a college-level course in poetry, although I have included what I consider to be a sufficient amount of information on poetry and the teaching of poetry. This book can best be described as one individual teacher's sharing of what he knows and loves best. So please, teachers . . . borrow . . . throw out. Adapt. Expand. Modify. Use and enjoy.

PART I
UNDERSTANDING POETRY

THE PURPOSE OF POETRY
Caretakers of the human experience . . .

SERVED ME WELL

As I looked and listened, it was as if I were seeing with different eyes—the colors so vivid, the trees and foliage so perfect. The rustling of the wind and the melody of distant birds came to me— as if, childlike, I were hearing them for the first time. Lines from e e cummings hummed themselves over and over in my mind.

now the ears of my ears awake and
now the eyes of my eyes are opened . . .

One of my favorite leisure activities is bicycle touring. I find long, slow-paced bicycle trips simply exhilarating. Pedaling miles from home, my bike saddles loaded with camping gear, my mind and body are freed from the yard that needs mowing, the overdue correspondence, the lessons that need preparation—the seemingly endless domestic and professional obligations.

While riding along a remarkably beautiful mountain pass, I once thought: What if, God forbid, I veered off this road, tumbled over the side, and landed with a broken arm in a heap of bike? I decided I would probably want a doctor to tend to my broken arm. Not a poet. Likewise I would appreciate someone with at least a mechanical aptitude—if not a certified bicycle repairman—to reassemble my bicycle. A poet wouldn't do. If it were a car hogging the road that caused my misfortune that afternoon, I would definitely prefer walking (or limping, who knows?) into court with a lawyer. A poet, more than likely, would be of no help.

But that very same afternoon, safe and intact as I rode, it was the poets and their work that proved special to me. Riding, my bike meandering like a contented stream through a winding valley, I felt as if I were more alive than I had ever been. It was as if all that was around me was caressing me. Bicycling over rivers and streams, which cars in their airtight sterility sped by, I could smell the fragrance of the water, hear it lap soothingly against its shore. The scent of nectar overwhelmed me. Looking around I could see the delicate shapes of the trees and foliage, and admire the blue-shadowed layering of the terrain in the distance and the perfectly composed sky. At times, I felt I could almost touch serenity in the world as it should be, feeling the sun's rays warming my face and shoulders.

I was open and receptive to the sheer sensations of everything around me, and it was poetry that enhanced and made so rich this experience. It was through poetry that I was first acquainted with much of what I was now experiencing. Poetry opens our minds to what is already around us; it teaches us to feel our world more intensely, more joyously.

For example, who, knowing Rachel Field's "Something Told the Wild Geese," can see a flock of geese crossing the sky in a gently rippling "V" as they head south, and not marvel at the sight, or nearly hear lines from the poem? Or who, after reading Frost's "Birches," can ever see a grove of bowing birches the way he saw it before reading the poem? Poems fix themselves within our minds like wonderful tastes in our mouths.

Without coming to know different poets' visions of nature I might, like the airtight car speeding over the bridge, never have been able to see and hear and taste and smell as I did that afternoon, or other afternoons, at other times, in other places. That afternoon I was swelling with Walt Whitman's poetic sense of the "open road."

Afoot and light-hearted I take to
*   the open road,*

Healthy, free, the world before me,
The long brown path before me
         leading wherever I choose.
. . .

You road I enter upon and look
         around, I believe you
     are not all that is here,
I believe that much unseen is
         also here.
. . .

You air that serves me with
         breath to speak!
You objects that call diffusion
     my meanings and give
     them shape!
. . .

The earth expanding right hand
         and left hand,
The picture alive, every part
     in its best light,
. . .

(WALT WHITMAN, "Song of the Open Road")

I was healthy and free, the world before me, seeing everything around me as a picture in its best light. It was as if a floodgate of images were released inside me. Along with Whitman there were other poets: Rachel Field and her word-paintings of nature, Carl Sandburg's "prairies," David McCord, Robinson Jeffers, Wendell Berry, David Wagoner, e e cummings, my beloved Robert Frost— the list could go on. All had contributed. All had helped my seeing the "unseen" that is also there. I had allowed their eyes to let me see.

Beyond the sensations of the natural world, other poets had given me avenues of personal reflection that afternoon—to wonder and think about "me," my purpose and place in the world, my sense of selfhood and of personal vision. I was leaving a secure and relatively comfortable teaching position to make my way as a storyteller and independent language arts consultant. Who would hire me? Would enough schools use me so that I could make my house payments? Could what talents I possess sustain me? The anxiety sometimes frightened me. But the poem my teaching faculty couldn't recognize a few years before gave me comfort. I was taking a "road less traveled" and, maybe, it could make "all the difference."

Yes, the poets were serving me well that afternoon.

So, too, each of the others I'd thought about could have served me well: The doctor, my medical needs. The mechanic, my need for transportation. The lawyer, my need for judicial fairness. But that afternoon it was the poets who rode with me.

STILL A PERSON

It may seem superfluous that someone who simply delights in poetry's pleasure would need to concern himself with its purpose. Does pleasure need a purpose? But in reality, there is always the hovering question of poetry's relevance in today's increasingly "high-tech" world.

What need is there for poetry, some might ask, in a society in which, as predicted by John Naisbett, author of *Megatrends*, seventy-five percent of all future jobs will involve computers? (Naisbett 1982, 27). Computers use computer language, which by its very nature and purpose is at odds with the poetic use of language. Computer language is command-oriented, invented to be used in a particularly programmed computer. At this point in computer technology, the *sound* of computer language is irrelevant. Poetic language is universal, expressive, abstract, and open to multi-interpretation. The sound of poetic language, or what the reader or listener hears in his or her head, is an essential part of the poetic experience. What purpose can one find for knowing a rhyming couplet in a world where it sometimes seems that literacy is being translated to mean computer literacy? What need is there for poems in a world being so thoroughly overtaken by technological media?

The answer to these questions is as basic as, say, you or me. For seated at the monitor screen of every computer with its "megachip" capacity for storing and retrieving unimaginable amounts of information, there is—you guessed it—still a person. A person with individual needs and concerns; a complicated person living in daily contact with other complicated persons in an ever-increasingly complicated world; a person who's capable of loving intensely and hating equally as vehemently; a person who needs to reflect, to make personal decisions, to accept or reject values, and to take certain courses of action; a person whose understanding of himself must be predicated on an understanding of where he came from;

a person with a vast spiritual capacity. Not a machine. A human—loving, experiencing—being.

SERIES OF EXPLANATIONS OF LIFE

Carl Sandburg said that poetry is a "series of explanations of life." And indeed, that is where poetry is of value, even to the person whose occupation seats him before the computer (Sandburg 1970, 318). For poetry is primarily concerned with the *experience* of living. Human beings, whether ancient hunters dressed in rawhide or technological engineers in three-piece suits, have always had the inner need to find meaning and purpose in their lives, to experience life as fully as they can with the greatest awareness of themselves and the world around them.

Poets through the ages have created, by means of their own resources, observations, and genius, poems that are capable of fulfilling the human need to live more fully and meaningfully—poems that beckon us to experience life; that allow our imaginations to be merged in another individual's vision; that heighten and enhance our perceptions of ourselves, as well as our *inner* selves.

In this, poetry is as relevant today as it has been throughout recorded history. The poet serves as a caretaker of the human experience. Poetry, Keats said, should appear almost as a remembrance of the reader's own unexpressed emotion or thought. All societies through all of history have given voice to their experiences in order to understand them, and by doing so have created some form of poetry. The poets have left a record of humankind's joys and loves, failings and misgivings, greatest accomplishments, and worst disasters. From this record modern human beings can come to sense their kinship with the past and their place in the world today, as well as to stretch their minds to the unimagined and, as yet, unattainable realms of the future.

Poetry is as much a part of human beings as is their cultural history. It is the gift of cultural memory. But we are not born understanding and appreciating this legacy. The gift must be taught, passed gently and joyfully from one generation to the next. To deprive individuals of an understanding of poetry, as of any art, is to deprive them of one of the most satisfying aspects of their own human nature. As Whitman said in "Song of Myself," they would miss an "endless unfolding of words of ages."

THE NATURE OF POETRY
...and guardians of the language

A WAY OF SAYING

Robert Frost was fond of referring to his oral reading of poems as "saying." "I'd like to say another poem for you," he would tell an audience. In his typical fashion, calling on as few words as possible, Frost, by using *say* instead of *read*, illuminated more about the very nature of poetry than a volume of scholarship. For poetry in its simplest terms is a way of *saying*.

Saying, unlike reading, implies *voice*.

Poetic voice beckons and even insists on being heard . . . not just decoded through the eyes and processed by our reading minds in an intellectual sense, but being heard through our ears. To read a poem well we must lift it off the page by means of our reading ears. Listening to poetry is the first thing I try to get across to beginning poetry readers. I have them cover their ears with their hands and let their eyes read a poem silently while they listen intensely inside their heads.

Could you hear what you were reading?
What did it sound like to you?

To this day I cannot simply read a poem. I find myself subvo-
calizing it or, if the situation allows, reading it aloud. Poets, or
poetry, that I have heard, either in live performance or on a recording, leave an auditory imprint on my mind. When I read the
same poetry, I hear it in the same voice that was imprinted on my
mind—the same pausing and hesitation, the same emphasis and
breath pattern. Having heard the late Montana poet Richard Hugo
many years ago, I cannot to this day even glance at his work without
hearing, deep within the canyons of my mind, his rich, melodic
voice, as if he were reading aloud over my shoulder.

An activity I've developed to use in my classes that stresses the
idea of learning to listen to a poem is called the "couplet completing
game." I take paired lines or stanzas of poetry and separate them
by writing them on different three-by-five-inch index cards. For
example, I use lines from Langston Hughes's poem, "Dreams" (see
Figure 2–1). I do the same type of thing with lines and stanzas from
many different poems. The children will be familiar with some; they
won't be with others. The cards are mixed up and one card is given
to each child. The object of the activity is to find the line or stanza
that goes with that card. The only rule is that you keep saying your
line aloud while listening to others saying their lines, until your ears
tell you you've found the line that goes with yours. Although the
activity may get loud and hectic, it forces the participants actually
to listen to how poetry sounds.

Its most unique characteristic

The importance of having youngsters hear poetry being read, or as
Frost would insist, said, is a vital first step to having them enjoy
poetry and supports an argument for having parents and teachers
read to children daily. Bill Martin Jr, author and innovative reading
consultant, states in many of his presentations that the unique characteristic of any word is its sound, which he says "fixes itself within
the fibers of the listener's mind."

Through its word-sounds, poetic language gains its dramatic vitality. The sounds of words are qualitatively different from their
printed form. Printed words may have one meaning or a couple of
possible meanings, but the sounds of those words orchestrated with

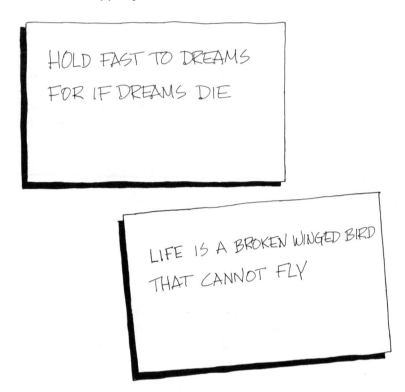

Figure 2–1

the sounds of other words create a poetic line that lingers in one's mind even after the eyes have left the page.

Words come to their full brilliance only in the creation of poetry. It is said that prose is made up of words in the best order, but poetry is made up of the best words in the best order. And those best words and best orders are predicated on word sounds, which even without a complete understanding of their meaning, can puzzle and delight us beautifully. One need only listen to a dramatic reading of Lewis Carroll's "Jabberwocky" to realize this. Words—normal, everyday words—in the hands of a poet, transcend the literal and can open in the mind of the reader an element of ecstasy.

In the way

Isn't it ironic, though, that the very quality that gives poetry its uniqueness, its power, and its beauty is the same quality that stands in the way of many beginning students' appreciation of it? Poetry appears as a mysterious, coded language that is the exclusive property of the teacher. The poet's way of saying, quite honestly, gets *in the way* of students' enjoyment of poetry.

Our youngsters today, from the moment they can distinguish between fantasy and reality, feel society's persistent push for the concrete, literal use of language.

Don't use baby talk. Talk like an adult!
Say exactly what you mean—no highfalutin' words!

Education adds its share, too:

Fill in the blank with the correct word—nothing else.

Any teacher who has taught for at least the last ten years with any ear at all for literature has noticed how watered-down the language of our textbooks has become. Pick up an old primer from the early 1900s and you'll see how rich was the language to which students of that day were exposed.

Thus the beginning student is assigned a poem. She reads it. She doesn't have the faintest idea what the poet is doing because she doesn't know what poetry is about. The words appear to her to be stumbling blocks getting in the way of the poem's meaning. "Mumbo Jumbo," she says. She has not learned to open up those aspects of her intelligence that allow her simply to feel, imagine, and experience. She assuredly has not listened to the poem. Perhaps it's even a poor poem in the first place.

Understandably, though, her mind tells her that this poem doesn't make sense. In fact, its not making sense makes her feel stupid. And who wants to feel stupid over something that doesn't make sense? She says she doesn't like the poem . . . and in the next breath she states that she doesn't like poetry.

A precious side of an individual might never be opened.

WORDS—THE POET'S OBSESSION

How then can I present what poetry is so that you can become a better reader of poetry? Or so that you can teach poetry to your students in a way that will allow them to become better readers of poetry? The most logical starting point would be the first thing that strikes your eye or meets your ear when reading any poem—the words.

Words. Words are the poet's obsession. He knows them inside and out. Where a word may mean one thing to you, to the poet the word is a wonderful, multi-dimensional phenomenon. He knows the sound, the texture, the movement, the flexibility of words. To him, words are as mystical as a perfectly struck chord of music.

The poet Dylan Thomas wrote in his *Notes on the Art of Poetry* that before he could read poems as a child he "had come to love just the words of them; the words alone." Words were to him

> as the notes of bells, the sound of musical instruments, the noises of wind, sea, and rain, the rattle of milk-carts, the clopping of hooves on cobbles, the fingering of branches on a window-pane, might be to someone, deaf from birth, who has miraculously found his hearing. (Thomas 1968, 316)

Is it any wonder that this child was to become one of our most celebrated lyric poets?

There is an enchanting, childlike quality in a poet's awareness of words. Like a child who loves jingles, rhymes, and nonsense sounds, the poet loves the harmony, melody, and rhythms that words can create. Listen to the qualities Mary O'Neill attributes to words:

> *Some words clink*
> *As ice in drink.*
> *Some move with grace*
> *A dance, a lace.*
> *Some sound thin:*
> *Wail, scream and pin.*
> *Some words are squat:*
> *A mug, a pot,*
> *And some are plump,*
> *Fat, round and dump.*
> *Some words are light:*
> *Drift, lift and bright.*
> *A few are small:*
> *A, is and all.*
> *And some are thick,*
> *Glue, paste and brick.*
> *Some words are sad:*
> *"I never had. . . . "*
> *And others gay:*
> *Joy, spin and play.*
> *Some words are sick:*
> *Stab, scratch and nick.*

Some words are hot:
Fire, flame and shot.
Some words are sharp,
Sword, point and carp.
And some alert:
Glint, glance and flirt.
Some words are lazy:
Saunter, hazy.
And some words preen:
Pride, pomp and queen.
Some words are quick,
A jerk, a flick.
Some words are slow:
Lag, stop and grow,
While others poke
As ox with yoke.
Some words can fly—
There's wind, there's high;
And some words cry:
"Goodbye . . .
Goodbye. . . . "

(MARY O'NEILL, "Feelings About Words")

Carl Sandburg also was infatuated with the nature of words:

. . . for words are made of syllables
and syllables, child, are made of air—
and air is so thin
   —air is the breath of God—
air is finer than fire or mist,
finer than water or moonlight,
finer than spider-webs in the moon,
finer than water-flowers in the morning:
   and words are strong, too,
   stronger than rocks or steel
   stronger than potatoes, corn, fish, cattle,
   and soft too,
   soft as the music of hummingbird-wings

(from "Little Girl, Be Careful What You Say")

Like painters who select specific colors and hues to evoke feelings in the viewers of their art, poets paint their poems with words and phrases that create the feelings they want their readers or listeners to experience. Notice the haunting mood the poet Jack Prelutsky creates simply with these words and phrases from his poem "The Dance of the Thirteen Skeletons":

> ... snow-enshrouded graveyard ...
> ... not a single soul is stirring ...
> ... distant bell tolls midnight ...
> ... spirits ...
> ... spectral show ...
> ... eerie circle ...
> ... penetrating breeze ...
> ... spindly fingers ...

The list could continue, but for the sake of your sleep tonight I'll not go on. A good exercise for young readers is to list the specific words they discover a poet has used to create a mood or feeling or setting for his readers—for example, the autumn words and phrases Dixie Wilson uses in her poem "The Mist and All," or the sea words and phrases found in John Masefield's "Sea-Fever."

An expression I am fond of using in my classes and workshops is "as the stars are to the heavens so words are to poems." This conveys well, if only metaphorically, the powerful importance of words to poetry. To reinforce this idea, I often have my students "star" the poems we are examining or draw a star around the individual words that give a poem or line of poetry its brilliance. With lines such as

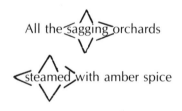

All the sagging orchards

steamed with amber spice

from Rachel Field's "Something Told the Wild Geese," I would want them to discover that the words "sagging" and "steamed" were specific word choices that made the line so vivid. By coming to recognize a poet's "star words," students move closer to noticing and eventually appreciating the art of poetry.

Transcends the literal

The poet's acute awareness of words and their qualities is more times than not a stumbling block to students' understanding of a poem. Students' reading minds want words simply to denote a specific meaning or, as the growing boy was told, to say what they mean. But the poet stretches his words by exploiting their connotations. Words in poetry can suggest more, beyond what they simply mean. By using the connotations of words poets can add a multiplicity of meaning to their work.

Notice, for example, how Edwin Arlington Robinson's word choices suggest more than they denote in the opening stanza of "Richard Cory":

> *Whenever Richard Cory went down town,*
> *We people on the pavement looked at him:*
> *He was a gentleman from sole to* crown,
> *Clean favored, and* imperially *slim.*

Robinson chose to use the word *crown* in the sense of the top of one's head in describing Richard Cory. He could have simply used *from head to foot* or, for that matter, *from top to bottom* to denote the same thing. But by using *crown* he suggests something beyond the exact meaning of the word. With *crown* he gives the impression of royalty that persists in the reader's mind. The same is true when he calls Cory *imperially slim* instead of, say, *really thin.* The suggestion of Cory's aristocratic nature is indelibly fixed on the reader's mind, although it is never exactly said.

One dimension of poetry's way of saying is this unique use of words. The poet says more than the simple meanings of his words. He uses the words along with their suggestive nature to create the feeling he wants his readers to experience. Beginning students might ask, "Well, why doesn't he just say what he wants? Why doesn't he say Richard Cory was a snobby aristocrat?" Because the poet wants the reader to sense what Richard Cory appeared to be, much like the people on the pavement in the poem responded to what Richard Cory *appeared* to be. Richard Cory appeared to have it all:

> *richer than a king;*
> *admirably schooled in every grace;*
> *he was everything.*

This sets up the shock the reader experiences, for those of you unfamiliar with the poem, when:

> *And Richard Cory, one calm summer night,*
> *Went home and put a bullet through his head.*

Packing light

Along with the poet's keen concern for how words sound and for their potential meaning, she is cautiously aware that words can become "excess verbal baggage" in a poem. I'm sure we've all, at one time or another, overpacked for a trip. We've said, "Well, let me see, I might need that" or "Might as well bring this along, too," until our car was filled to the grill. Much of what we packed we never really needed or, for that matter, used. Unlike us, a poet doesn't simply pack words she doesn't need into the poem. She is forever chipping away at unnecessary words, much like a sculptor chips away at a block of marble until he has left just what he needs to make his statement.

I heard the poet Diane Wakoski once state in a writing class that she pares down her first drafts by ninety percent in the process of creating her poems. It is this condensed use of language that may throw off a beginning reader. A poem may not appear to explain itself. It just appears "out of nowhere" on the page, waiting to be discovered. I've always jokingly said that the reason students come to want everything explained is that they are used to teachers, and teachers notoriously explain everything thirty times (a hazard of the profession, I suppose).

Because a poem is pared down to perfectly selected words, every single word counts. If a reader skips or misses a word, it may mean an incomplete image or an unintelligible thought. Our students are often careless readers. "I'm done," one will shout, after only skimming a piece, "but I don't understand a word of it." Helping students come to understand the condensed language that a poet uses is the first of many necessary steps into the art of poetry.

Perhaps "The Written Words," by an anonymous writer, best demonstrates how a poem can be more effective when its "excess verbal baggage" is left at home.

A

The spoken or written word
Should be as clean as a bone,
As clear as is the light,
As firm as is a stone.
Two words will never serve
As well as one alone.

B

The written word
Should be as clean as bone,
Clear as light
Firm as stone.
Two words are not
As good as one.

Do what they do with words

Is it any surprise, then, that reading a mature poem can become a frustrating task for youngsters? Their reading minds, accustomed to years upon years of prose, have come to expect a simple sub-ject/predicate ordering of words within a sentence. Poetry follows no such pattern. The cogs of their comprehension mechanisms have come to operate by loading in the denotative meanings of individ-ual, isolated words. Poetry uses words in different and difficult ways. Their eyes and ears, having grown comfortable well within the bounds of the paragraph, are caught off-guard with poetry's unusual use of sound and shape.

But such is the nature of the art!

And as such it is an art that can be explored—explored and examined creatively and meaningfully in the classroom so that chil-dren come to see poetry not as a mysterious, foreign language but as a different use of their own language, a language that they can understand and that can bring them new joys and different sorts of insights. Many times during the year, I would pass out to my class a "way-of-saying" sheet. The sheet was simply a gathering of four or five memorable lines of poetry taken from their books or from the poem we were studying. Next to the line, I would leave a space for them to paraphrase the line in a way a non-poet would write it. The kids might, for example, take the lines in Rachel Field's "The Green Fiddler": "Twilight came stealing / from tree to tree" and write, "It got darker" (see Figure 2–2).

Not only did we have a lot of fun with the unexpected answers, but I also felt I was helping the children cultivate a sensitivity to the "craft" behind poetry. I wanted them to come to see, through activities such as this, how vivid in imagery and rich in sound language could be when in the hands of a poet. In order to open

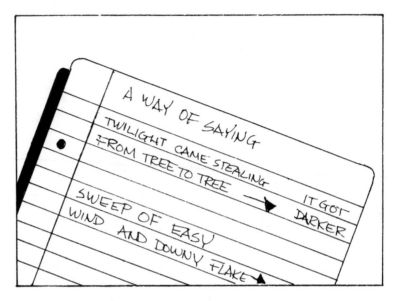

Figure 2–2

children to the exploration of poetry we must help them see the ways poets do what they do with words, the ways poets use words to create what they want to create in their poetry. The next chapter will examine just that.

THE ELEMENTS OF POETRY
. . . words in performance

Many writers talk about poetry as "words performing." One only needs to hear a captivating reading of Stephen Vincent Benét's well-known poem "The Mountain Whippoorwill" to see how masterfully his words actually create the sound of fiddle music. Poets such as Benét design their work so that the melodic quality of the words—their rhythms and sound patterns—create a desired effect. Meaning and melody in the poem become one. A verbal music is made.

I have often taught my students about poetry by having them imagine that they are in the top bleachers at a circus looking down toward the acts taking place on the floor.

"What do you see?" I ask them.

"Different rings," they say.

"And what is going on in each ring?"

"In one ring a tiger is jumping through a hoop," they'll suggest, "and in another a man is juggling, and in another clowns are performing."

"Well, that's sorta like poetry," I tell them, "only with poetry, rather than having tigers, jugglers, and clowns performing, you have words performing. And just as the circus has many acts all going on at once, in poems the words are all performing at once as you read or listen to a poem. Some words are rhyming, some are setting up a rhythm, while some might be posing as a startling image. Poetry is like a three-ring circus of word performances."

I'll examine in this chapter what can go on in each of the different rings of poetry.

RHYTHM—HEARTBEAT OF THE POEM

The underlying feature of poetry as performance must be its rhythm. Rhythm is the pulse of a poetic piece: its life beat, its vitality. Jim Trelease, author of the popular *The Read-Aloud Handbook*, contends that the first sound a child hears is a poem of the rhythmic beating of its mother's heart (Trelease 1982, 61).

Rhythm is a basic principle of all life. We breathe in rhythm; our bodies maintain a rhythm; our voices sustain rhythm; the world proceeds with the rhythm of the seasons. The waxing and waning of the moon, the pull and push of oceanic tides, the movement and migration of birds and animals—all are rhythmic.

Rhythm, whether with a regular beat such as a cadence or an irregular pattern, shoulders the poem, gives it movement and vigor. Children's natural linguistic passions lock on to rhythm before anything else in a poem. God only knows how many hamburgers have been sold under the watchful cadence of "two all-beef patties, special sauce, lettuce, cheese, pickles, onions, on a sesame-seed bun."

Very young children delight in the sheer, rhythmic fun of the nonsense verse of Mother Goose.

> *Hickory, dickory dock!*
> *The mouse ran up the clock;*
> *The clock struck one,*
> *And down he run,*
> *Hickory, dickory dock.*

Rhythm is contagious in both verbal chant and physical movement. Any good primary teacher can have the class singing, clapping, chanting, and gesturing with any rhythmic poem.

Rhythmic structuring of a poem gives it its flow, its shifts, and its melodic direction, so that the poet can conduct the language much like a symphony conductor conducts with his baton. I often have

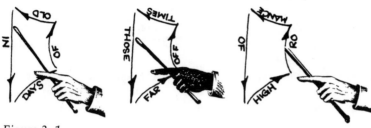

Figure 3–1

youngsters discover how a conductor might use his baton at the podium if he were conducting a poem. Lines from a poem like Robert S. Oliver's "The Toad"

In days of old, those far off times / Of high romance... /

might look something like the illustration in Figure 3–1.

Rhythm can also function to heighten the reader's attention or suggest the action of a poem. Notice how David McCord's rhythm in his classic, "The Pickety Fence," creates the sound of a stick being run along a picket fence.

The pickety fence
The pickety fence
Give it a lick it's
The pickety fence
Give it a lick it's
A clickety fence
Give it a lick it's
A lickety fence
Give it a lick
Give it a lick
Give it a lick
With a rickety stick
Pickety
Pickety
Pickety
Pick

Dinosaur species

For those of you who still have your faded college notes on the elements of poetry and are wondering why I've failed to mention ideas such as meter, and stressed and unstressed syllables in relation to rhythm, let me explain. First, strict metrical prosodies with their mind-boggling terminology—anapestic, dactylic, and spondaic (better suited for the naming of bizarre dinosaur species)—are well beyond the intended scope of this book. Second, and please don't tell my Poetry 101 teacher, to this day I can't figure out the syllabification of a line of poetry, much less correctly name it.

Focusing our teaching attention on the likes of iambic pentameter leads us into the age-old argument about whether the in-depth analysis of the technical aspects of poetry enhances children's (or, for that matter, anybody's) understanding and eventual appreciation of poetry. Although I would be the first one to stand up for the idea that kids be exposed to all that poetry offers, I wonder if our efforts could be better spent in ways other than counting stressed and unstressed syllables. I suggest that this type of activity might tend to defeat what we want to accomplish.

Poetry, I feel, should remain, as much as possible, an aesthetic experience for children. My rule of thumb for young kids is

> *if it flows on your*
> *tongue like candy*
> *and into your ear*
> *like music . . .*
> *it's poetic.*

Regardless, I might add, of whether its accentual syllabic prosody contains qualitative or normative accentual syllabic verse. Not once in my experience have I found children becoming overly fond of syllabic verse, but I have seen kids fall in love with a poem.

Rhythmical waves

Still it's important to have children see that the rhythm of a poem's lines is part of what makes it poetry, and that there is a flow of high and low sounds within a line. I like to have kids discover the rhythmic flow of a poem by talking about it in terms of the waves in the ocean. The model of waves with their slow build-up and crest presents a picture for seeing these high and low sounds. A line taken from "Wiggly Giggles," by Stacy Jo Crossen and Natalie Anne Covell, can be presented this way.

> *I've got the wiggly-wiggles today . . .*

I ask the kids,

Figure 3–2

Now, using your own ear, put these words on the picture of the waves. Which words (or sounds) would be at the top of the wave with the heaviest sound? Which are softer sounds that build up the side of the wave?

Using their own intuitive sense of what sounds right, the children can easily discover the rhythm of these lines graphically (see Figure 3–2). We read the poem together, hearing the ebbing and flowing sounds the poet intended, and we can leave the discussion of metric feet for another day.

It's also beneficial to allow children to create their own activities to discover the rhythmical impulse of poetic language. I might present lines such as these:

1. *A horse and a flea and three blind mice*
    Sat on a curbstone chewing ice.

    (from ''Whoops,'' author unknown)

2. *Moses supposes his toses are roses*
    But Moses supposes erroneously.

    (from ''Moses,'' author unknown)

I have teams of four or five youngsters create a variety of activities to sensitize their own ears to different rhythms. They share their rhythm activities with the class.

RHYME—THE GOLDEN THREAD

Like rhythm, rhyme is also a performing aspect of poetry to which children respond. Although all poems do not need or use rhyme, when it is used, it sculptures the poem and provides the eye and ear with a harmonious predictability. It weaves the lines and stanzas together to create a cohesive whole.

It is my impression that with school children we have overdone the idea that a poem doesn't have to rhyme. Often when I'm working in a school with a group of youngsters, I will ask them what they know about this thing "poetry." "It doesn't have to rhyme," they chorus, with the same autocratic conviction of "You must *always* look both ways before crossing a street." And they are right—a poem doesn't have to rhyme. But when it does, and does so with grace and meaning, a difficult word-feat is accomplished.

The late poet John Ciardi pointed out in an article for *Saturday Review* that the English language is a relatively trying one with which to use rhyme. While the French or Italian poet has many words that rhyme with one another, the English-speaking poet does not. His pool of potential rhyming words is by comparison quite shallow (Ciardi 1958, 13–15). Therefore, when he uses rhyme successfully, he has, in a sense, beaten the odds and should score high on individual word performance. Perhaps rather than making sure we hammer down the idea that poems don't have to rhyme we should come to see that rhyme is one of the possible ways in which words can perform. I encourage my students, when they use rhyme in their own poetry, to discover "rare rhymes" and to try not to use "other people's rhymes"—rhymes that they hear all the time.

The popular and easily the most widely read children's author—the immortal Dr. Seuss—uses wonderfully uncanny rhymes in all his books. Whenever I read or recite a Dr. Seuss story the children are all so familiar with its delightful rhyme that it would take rolls of masking tape to prevent them from joining in full unison every chance they get.

As a storyteller I often recite longer poems, so I know firsthand how the rhyme gives the poem cohesion. While reciting a tightly rhymed poem, such as a ballad, I occasionally miss a line or forget a clause. I can almost feel the whole structure of the poem collapsing in my throat. Without that predictable rhyme at the end of the phrase, the whole stanza falls apart as if a leg of the poem has been pulled out from underneath it.

With younger children I explain rhyme as the poet's "golden

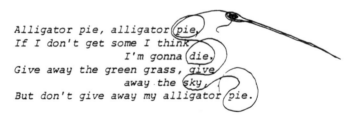

```
Alligator pie, alligator pie,
If I don't get some I think
                I'm gonna die.
Give away the green grass, give
            away the sky,
But don't give away my alligator pie.
```

Figure 3–3

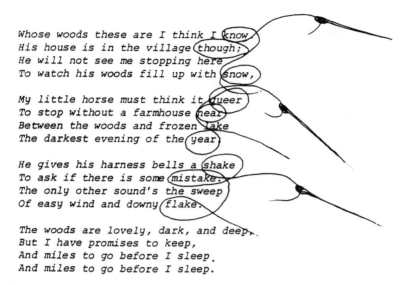

```
Whose woods these are I think I know
His house is in the village though;
He will not see me stopping here
To watch his woods fill up with snow,

My little horse must think it queer
To stop without a farmhouse near
Between the woods and frozen lake
The darkest evening of the year

He gives his harness bells a shake
To ask if there is some mistake.
The only other sound's the sweep
Of easy wind and downy flake.

The woods are lovely, dark, and deep,
But I have promises to keep,
And miles to go before I sleep.
And miles to go before I sleep.
```

Figure 3–4

thread." In poems such as Dennis Lee's "Alligator Pie," we can thread the first stanza (see Figure 3–3).

Continuing with the idea of a golden thread, notice the double overlapping pattern in Frost's "Stopping by Woods on a Snowy Evening." Interweaving the first, second, and last lines of the stanzas, and the third line of each stanza with the first of the following stanza, he has created a memorable effect (see Figure 3–4).

In my poetry-writing workshops, I've told the children not to let rhyme wear a "general's uniform" and order their poems around, but to remember what Robert Frost said (here rephrased): "for him writing poetry without rhyme or meter would be like playing tennis without a net" (Lathem and Thompson 1972, 415).

SOUND PATTERNS—FINE POINTS OF A WORD PERFORMANCE

Along with the rhythm and possibly rhyme, the poet may use sound patterns to accentuate what she is doing in the poem. In her study of children's poetry preferences, Ann Terry stated that the three poetic elements most popular with younger children are rhyme, rhythm, and sound patterns (Terry 1972, 20). Sound patterns such as alliteration, assonance, and onomatopoeia are effective in creating unusual and ear-catching sound patterns to which children joyfully respond.

By using alliteration, the repetition of beginning consonants, poets can tie two words together and underscore some good linguistic humor. Here are names from the poem "Ten Kinds" by Mary Mapes Dodge:

Winnie Whiney
Fannie Fibber
Kitty Kissem
Tillie Tattle

Do you remember the fun of alliteration in this familiar tongue twister?

Peter Piper picked a peck
of pickled peppers.

A way to have children begin to notice alliteration is to have them put colored checks over the repeating consonant sounds. In the last line of Carolyn Wells's poem "The Tutor," for example, the youngsters would put checks over the *t* sound:

Or to tutor two tooters to toot?

Assonance is much like alliteration except that it is the repetition of vowel sounds. It can have the same charming effect. Here are some examples of assonance taken from Irene McLeod's "Lone Dog":

. . . lean dog, keen dog . . .
. . . rough dog, tough dog . . .
. . . bad dog, mad dog . . .
. . . sleek dog, meek dog . . .

Sometimes a poet will use onomatopoeia, or words that imitate the thing or action they are associated with, to capture his reader's attention. Robert Service's classic line from "The Cremation of Sam McGee" is a good example. After stuffing Sam McGee into the flaming furnace, his partner leaves because he "didn't like to hear him *sizzle* so." The word *sizzle* sounds like what poor Sam was doing: burning. Kids, with their marvelously irreverent humor, never fail to catch this flaming onomatopoeia!

When working with younger kids, I find that the sound pattern created by alliteration and assonance can be made more vivid by using color. Alliteration and assonance in effect produce a sound ripple through a poem similar to the ripple created when you toss

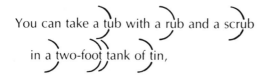

Figure 3–5

a pebble into a still body of water. The repeated sound ripples through a line or the entire body of the poem. To help children see this I often have them color-code a poem with bright-colored highlighter pens or crayons. In Sir Edward Parry's "The Kind of Bath for Me," for instance, I have the kids color the *u* sound in the first line with red and the alliterated *t* sound in the second line with another color. Eventually they can color the entire poem (see Figure 3–5). By doing this the kids can not only hear the sound pattern created, but also see the sound rippling on the paper. We can then explore the poem's repeated sounds and see what rhythms they create by clapping our hands at each colored bar. By hearing and seeing, we can experience the effect of a poem's sound pattern.

REPETITION—A POEM'S HANDLE

One of my favorite classical music pieces is Ravel's *Bolero*. Even before Blake Edwards's 1978 movie *10* made a household word of *Bolero* (along with some visual associations I don't believe Ravel ever intended), I was utterly intrigued with it. If you're not familiar with the piece, I'll attempt to talk about it from my nonexistent musical background. But I'd almost prefer that you put my book aside for a couple of hours while you run to the local record shop or lending library for a recording.

At any rate, the entire work is built around one easily recognizable melody that is repeated throughout. The melody in musical terms is, I believe, quite simple and extremely "hummable." The piece starts very quietly and almost innocently. Slowly but progressively with each repetition, however, more instrumental support is added to the melody. Each musical variation brings more vitality and intensity as the melody builds higher and higher.

By the end of the piece that same melody has built up to a powerful, nearly ecstatic, intensity that all but consumes you. I defy anyone to listen to a well-produced symphonic presentation of *Bolero* and not find that melody pounding inside his or her head by the end of it.

The repetition that shapes *Bolero* is like the repetition that can be found in poetry, although not always with the same intensity. Poets will often repeat a phrase, a line, or even an entire stanza. Used effectively, a repeated line can emphasize a feeling or an idea of which the poet wants the reader to be particularly aware. A refrain can establish an echoing or chorusing effect within the lines—drawing the listener into the poem. Christina Rossetti's seemingly simple little poem "Who Has Seen the Wind?" does just that by repeating the opening line in each of its stanzas and almost doing the same thing in its second lines.

> *Who has seen the wind?*
>   *Neither I nor you:*
> *But when the leaves hang trembling,*
>   *The wind is passing through.*

> *Who has seen the wind?*
>   *Neither you nor I:*
> *But when the leaves bow down their heads,*
>   *The wind is passing by.*

On a first reading one might not notice the shift she quietly puts into the second stanza by switching the sequence of "I nor you." Her repetition and near-repetition work well to create a very tightly constructed poem.

Repetition can be used to cast a spell as well. One can almost feel the searching, longing effect the repeated words "where is/are" create in David McCord's "Where."

> *Where is that little pond I wish for?*
> *Where are those little fish to fish for?*
> *Where is my little rod for catching?*
> *Where are the bites I'll be scratching?*
> *Where is my rusty reel for reeling?*
> *Where is my trusty creel for creeling?*
> *Where is the line for which I'm looking?*
> *Where are those handy hooks for hooking?*
> *Where is the worm I'll have to dig for?*
> *Where are the boots that I'm too big for?*
> *Where is my boat for rowing?*

Where is . . . ?
Well, anyway, it's snowing.

Numerous examples of the varied uses of repetition appear in children's poetry. One need only thumb through *The Random House Book of Poetry* (selected by the poet Jack Prelutsky) to see how many favorite children's poems use some sort of repetition. The repeated line or phrase becomes a handle that kids can easily hold onto while opening a poem's door. Like the effect of musical phrases in *Bolero*, the repetition of lines in a poem draws children into its movement and design.

When I am storytelling with just about any age group of youngsters, I make it a habit to teach them the repeating line or refrain so they can chorus in when I come to that part. For example, James Whitcomb Riley's "The Raggedy Man" has this line at the end of every stanza:

Raggedy! Raggedy! Raggedy Man!

When I recite the poem I have the youngsters chorus in with me.

Even some stories have a poetic refrain that allows kids to become a part of the story. Wanda Gág's delightful classic, *Millions of Cats*, repeats a number of times the lines:

Cats here, cats there,
Cats and kittens everywhere,
Hundreds of cats
Thousands of cats
Millions and billions and trillions of cats.

The kids chorus the lines with me during the story and also, to the dismay of their less-appreciative teachers, throughout the rest of the day. Repetition in poetry draws the chanting minds of children into the realm of the poem so that other aspects of the poem may be brought to life.

SPATIAL DESIGN—WORDS AT PLAY ON PAPER

Perhaps one of the most overlooked aspects of "words-in-performance" is the arrangement and placement of the printed words of a poem on the page itself. The spacing or nonspacing between words, the overall picture or shape created by the arrangement of the words of the poem, the use of indentation and punctuation, and the location of uppercase letters—these are all as much a part of the poet's design as the word choices themselves.

One of the most attractive features of the very popular *Sounds of Language* reading series originally published by Holt, Rinehart & Winston is that its typography puts a great emphasis on the creative and intriguing use of lettering. Its poems, and stories for that matter, vary in shape and design on the page. Rather than always following a left-to-right print pattern, words in a *Sounds of Language* book may swirl in a circular design; letters may explode on the page in enormous size or bold print, or shrink to a quiet whisper. The lettering is often integrated into the illustration of the page.

Examples of this are found throughout the series. From the text, *Sounds of a Distant Drum*, the words of David McCord's poem "Five Little Bats,"

> *Five little bats flew out of the attic:*
> *Five little bats all acrobatic*
> *One little bat flew through the city,*
> *One little bat was flitting pretty.*
> *One little bat flew round the gable,*
> *One little bat was not flight able.*
> *One little bat flew in and out of*
> *something or other, I haven't a doubt of*
> *That, or that five little bats erratic*
> *Flew back in and are now up attic.*

follow rolling, flowing lines that visually mimic the rising and falling of the voice when the lines of the poem are read aloud. The beautifully lettered design, created by Ray Barber, challenges the children's tongues to read the lines with a lilt, the poem's words rolling out of their mouths like bats out of an attic. The visual design of the poem's words fascinates the reader's eyes as it directs the reader's voice.

Bill Martin Jr, senior author of the series, explains in the accompanying teacher's guide that using intriguing printing designs encourages the readers "to explore the page of print" and to discover how language can play on a page (Martin and Brogan 1972, TE101). The shape and design of a poem are an important part of the experience of the poem. To read relentlessly from the first word to the last, never letting your eyes take in the visual design of the poem, diminishes some of its beauty and meaning. Poets for adults also use designs with their words. For example, Dylan Thomas's

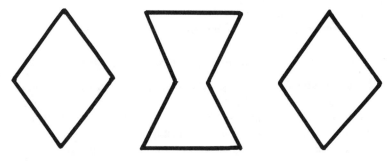

Figure 3–6

poem "Vision and Prayer," which is beautifully written and designed with two alternating and interlocking shapes (see Figure
3–6).

Eyeballing the poem

I often have younger children trace the structure of a poem with
their fingers to help them see the poem's physical shape. I want
them to "see" the poem as a whole unit made up of parts. I help
them discover some of the poet's design by asking:

> *How many longer lines are there?*
> *What kind of thoughts are in the longer lines?*
> *How many parts (stanzas) make up this poem?*
> *Do each of the different parts have the same shape?*
> *Would one of the parts fill the same space as another part?*
> *Close your eyes and trace in the air with your arms the shape of
> the poem and its parts.*
> *Now, keeping the shape in mind, let's read the poem together.*

Getting children to develop the habit of looking at the parts of a
poem, their functions, and their relationship to the poem's meaning
is sometimes a difficult task. With older kids, I take advantage of
their irreverent sense of humor and have them take out one of their
eyeballs (using their imaginations, mind you) and roll it over the
page, exploring the visual aspects of the poem before even beginning to read it. While their eyeballs are mischievously searching
the page, I talk:

> *Trace the shape. Any longer spaces between words?*
> *Any words getting scrunched together?*

Where's the bold print?
How about capitals? Punctuation?
Anything different?
Any words drooling down the page? Stretching across the page?

After we have read the poem, having returned our eyeballs to their rightful sockets, the natural question is Why? Why are the words arranged as they are? How do their shapes and placement relate to the meaning and intention of the poet?

Take, for example, one of e e cummings's unusual poems:

In Just-
spring   when the world is mud-
luscious the little
lame balloonman

whistles   far   and wee

and eddieandbill come
running from marbles and
piracies and it's
spring

when the world is puddle-wonderful

the queer
old balloonman whistles
far   and   wee
and bettyandisbel come dancing

from hop-scotch and jump-rope and

it's
spring
and
*   the*

*   goat-footed*

balloonMan   whistles
far
and
wee

By "eyeballing" this poem, youngsters discover how words can play on paper. They notice how word spacing can be telescoped in phrases like "whistles   far   and wee," and compressed in "ed-dieandbill" and "bettyandisbel." While rolling their eyes over the paper, kids will notice the use and nonuse of capitals (just "eddieandbill" and "bettyandisbel"). By examining the design of the poem, they discover the pacing of the poem. The "whistles (*pause*) far (*pause*) and wee" is drawn out while "eddieandbill" is said quickly, in one breath. Here is a poem whose basic understanding and appreciation require that the reader explore the printed words' performance.

Concrete poems

Poems demonstrating the most obvious word design are called *concrete* poems. In concrete poems, the words are arranged into the actual shape of the content of the poem. For example, "The Drippings of a Drop" by an anonymous author is shaped as a drop of water. (See Figure 3–7.)

The Drippings of a Drop

```
                      ɔ
                      s
                     dr
                    splɛ
                   prinl
                  ɟrip drc
                 Ʌdribble
                rɑin splash
               tinkle  drip s
              splash drop rɑi.
              ndrip  tinkle slasr
              ping  drip sprinkle ι
              splash drool pong drc
              tinkle drip ping sprink.
             ι splash drop drool poing
             ꞉ ping sprinkle dribble spl
             ι drizzle drip splash drops
             ʒ poing sprinkle ping drool
             p splash drip toing tinkles
             ꞉ drool sprinkle drizzle ti
             ιl ping tinkle splash wosh
             ꞉ poing dribble bubble sʳ
              ꞉ toing drool drip wisʰ
               ·ol splash toing pinɡ
               ˡe sprinkle droɾ·
                ˡ drip dɾ·
```

Anonymous

Figure 3–7

Frank Lloyd Wright of word designs

But concrete poems are not the only ones in which word arrangement adds to the meaning of the poem. e e cummings, as you've
probably guessed, might be considered the Frank Lloyd Wright of
word designs. His wild and nearly hieroglyphic designs may make
his poetry more difficult to read, but one certainly can't overlook
his artistry. Look at this piece:

!blac
k
agains
t

(whi)

te sky
?t
rees whic
h fr

om droppe

d

,
le
af

a:;go

e
s wh
lrll
n

.g

Now think of a leaf falling to the ground, sunlight glancing
off it as it flutters downward. The letters and fractured words
dropping down the page can be roughly visualized and interpreted as: black against white sky; trees from which dropped
leaf goes whirling.

Too advanced for a child? Perhaps. But isn't that the same type
of thing an eight-year-old is attempting here?

Aspens . . .
  twirling
    flying
      falling
from the sky
  gold
    yellow
      brown
like colors melted
in the ground

I encourage kids to take both published poems and their own poetry and make designs just with the words. Poems such as Alvin Tresselt's "White Snow, Bright Snow," for example, come out as carefully crafted art projects—here words are drawn like snowflakes drifting down the page. The design aids meaning and encourages the appreciation of the poetry.

"Building blocks" of understanding

Encouraging youngsters to see the overall design of a poem helps them understand the poem in its "completeness." A problem I sense that children have is thinking a poem just starts with the first word and ends when the poet is tired and puts his pencil down. They don't see an overall design within the structure of the poem. I often talk about lines and stanzas as building blocks. I ask the kids to discover how the blocks of a poem can be shown on paper.

Going back to the marvelous little piece, "The Kind of Bath for Me" (here in its entirety), I have children think of each couplet, or pair of lines, as square blocks.

You can take a tub with a rub and a scrub
  in a two-foot tank of tin,
You can stand and look at the whirling brook
  and think about jumping in;
You can chatter and shake in the cold black lake,
  but the kind of bath for me,
Is to take a dip from the side of a ship,
  in the trough of the rolling sea.
You may lie and dream in the bed of a stream
  when an August day is dawning,

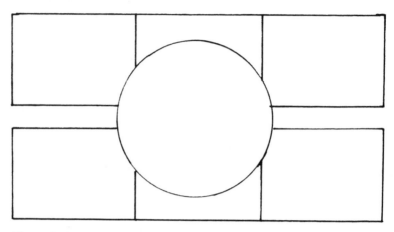

Figure 3–8

> *Or believe 'tis nice to break the ice*
>   *on your tub of a winter morning;*
> *You may sit and shiver beside the river,*
>   *but the kind of bath for me,*
> *Is to take a dip from the side of a ship*
>   *in the trough of the rolling sea.*
>
>   (SIR EDWARD PARRY, "The Kind of Bath for Me")

Then I ask,

> *Now, given this design, can you match the lines with their blocks?*
> *(See Figure 3–8.)*

The kids soon see how the first three blocks, or the first six lines, form the top rectangular shape. "A stanza!" I proclaim. The refrain is its own box, and the following six lines make another rectangle. "Stanza number two!" I exclaim. Finally, since the refrain is a repeated pair of lines, it's shared by both stanzas—hence the overlapping circle in the center of the design.

IMAGERY—SOURCE OF THE FLOW

If rhythm, rhyme, and other poetic devices act to carry a poem's movement and fluency through the listener's ear to his mind, then it is the poem's imagery that affixes itself to the walls of that listener's mind. Poetry that is read well captures and preserves scenes and feelings, and allows its readers to reexperience those same scenes and sensations at will. While we experience our daily lives directly through our senses, we experience the imagery in poetry through the senses of the mind's imagination.

A reader's ability to see, smell, and touch a poem is due to the success of the poem's imagery. Poets search for particular, specific details that will appeal to the reader's own senses—"tasting, touching, hearing, seeing, breathing," as e e cummings has said. Poetic imagery strives to leave an unshakable impression on the reader. Imagery, in a sense, is the clear water spring from which the poem's river flows.

I often tell youngsters that good images are thumbtacked to the backs of their heads on skinny strips of paper. I suspect that there isn't an American alive who doesn't have "He had a broad face and a little round belly / That shook, when he laughed, like a bowl full of jelly" thumbtacked to the back of his or her head. Here are a couple of striking images that have affixed themselves permanently in my mind.

With a face most hair, and the dreary stare
of a dog whose day is done,

    (ROBERT SERVICE, "The Shooting of Dan McGrew")

When I see birches bend to left and right
Across the lines of straighter, darker trees,
I like to think some boy's been swinging them.

    (ROBERT FROST, "Birches")

All the sagging orchards
Steamed with amber spice,

    (RACHEL FIELD, "Something Told the Wild Geese")

The list could go on and on.

In the same way, I try to help kids find and retain memorable poetic images from the poetry we study together. One requirement I have when we are examining a poem is that the students underline with colored pencils the image or images that most appeal to them. They write down these gatherings of phrases and lines and keep them in their poetry notebooks. I also have them on the lookout for poetic images in prose pieces. One of my favorite Jane Yolen stories, "Once a Good Man," from her collection *The Hundredth Dove and Other Tales*, contains this poetic jewel,

the wind feathering her wings,

embedded in the sentence, "So the Chief Angel flew down, the wind feathering her wings, and landed at the foot of the mountain." From time to time my class and I will pull out our poetry notebooks and share our favorite images.

> *Okay, let's have it. Who's got an image to share?*
> *Marvelous. (Big applause) Who's next?*
> *Spit 'em out now . . .*
> *I know you've got some hidden images in those notebooks.*

It's not only readers of poetry who hold on to selected moments of poetic imagery. Poets themselves savor selected images within their own works. I recall Byrd Baylor, author of such wonderful poetic renderings of the desert southwest as *The Desert Is Theirs, Desert Voices*, and *The Way to Start a Day*, saying that she couldn't pick her favorite book from those she'd written. She could, however, easily find the four or five lines within each of her books that were the ones she held on to and favored.

I encourage students to "trust their own ears" and find what appeals to them as individuals. What I keep in the "poetry drawers" of my mind is unique to me and my experiences. What they hold on to should be unique to them and their experiences.

A class activity to do with images is to take an unfamiliar poem, copy it without its title, and see if the class can guess the title by looking at its images. Can you guess the title of this old Alfred Tennyson poem?

> *He clasps the crag with crooked hands;*
> *Close to the sun in lonely lands,*
> *Ringed with the azure world, he stands.*
>
> *The wrinkled sea beneath him crawls;*
> *He watches from his mountain walls,*
> *And like a thunderbolt he falls.*

With image clues such as "clasps . . . with crooked hands" and "like a thunderbolt he falls," perhaps you, as well as your class, can guess the title "The Eagle."

Younger kids like to take visual images from poems and express them artistically. My second graders created a huge mural after listening to Rachel Field's "The Green Fiddler." Each child selected one mental picture from the poem and with crayons, pencils, and Magic Markers took to illustrating that moment. I then had the opportunity to show the children how it was the poet's words that created the picture in their heads. The child who chose, for example, to illustrate the hill where the girl in the poem met the little elfin fiddler was shown how words such as

. . . humpbacked hill . . .
. . . where trees crowd thick
   and black . . .

helped create the picture in her mind.

The imagery of a well-written poem begs to be preserved. It entices us to enter into the world created by the poem, to see life as the poet created it, to abandon our ordinary perceptions and experiences, and to carry with us the vision of the world as the poet sees it.

METAPHORIC DIMENSIONS—TWO FRIENDS MEETING

Like the connotative use of language, metaphoric thought is an activity we are inclined toward as children, but are gently pushed away from as we mature. As children we are comfortable seeing the moon as a smiling face, stars as blinking eyes, and clouds as gobs of white cotton candy. In a sense, children make metaphors of the entire world around them. They explain unfamiliar things by combining qualities of things they know. A strawberry when first introduced to a child might be called a "ladybug candy," for instance. The child has taken the strawberry's red color and shape and its sweetness and combined it with the red color and spots of a ladybug and the sweet taste of candy.

As we grow up, however, and our vocabularies become more precise and literal, we shy away from our metaphor-making capacities. In fact, most studies, as well as our own teaching experience, tell us that figurative language (metaphors, similes, and personification) tends to make poetry more difficult for children to understand, many times resulting in a dislike of poetry. Older students want words that accurately describe things. Consequently, while their vocabularies expand, an aspect of their language diminishes. The richness and flavor gained by metaphor are lost. The moon becomes a revolving minor satellite, stars are gaseous planets, and clouds . . . well, they become indicators of rain.

What I have discovered is that children are frequently asked to memorize what similes and metaphors are, without really seeing that they are simply one of a writer's tricks to make words perform. "A simile," they will quote, "is the comparison of two different things using the words *as, like,* or *than.* A metaphor is . . . " and so on. Metaphor and his two sisters, simile and personification, are better viewed as tools poets use to create memorable and lasting images in their work. Using a metaphor is like bringing two of your friends together for the first time. The meshing of their personalities can create an immediate and memorable association. Edna St. Vincent Millay did so in "The Ballad of the Harp Weaver" when she combined the fierceness of a howling wolf with the sound the wind can make.

> *A wind with a wolf's head*
> *Howled about our door,*

To this day I cannot hear a violent wind and not think of a wolf's head.

Having children fold three-by-five-inch index cards in half so that they open up like the wings of butterflies, and then draw and color the two halves with a variety of similes and metaphors can create a colorful wall display of metaphoric dimensions as well as helping train youngsters to "net" the metaphors that "flutter" through their readings. Metaphors children discover themselves strike an image that is likely to last because they will respond with their emotional side.

In my classes there were a couple of ways you could bring a lot of attention upon yourself. First, you could have a birthday and bring chocolate-covered donuts, Mr. Denman's favorite, as treats. Or, second, you could use metaphoric language in your writing. Since society seemed to be pushing kids toward literal language, in my poetry classes I have reversed the trend.

> *Class, slap 'em pencils to your desks. You just gotta hear this mega-wonderful metaphor of Julie's!*

When children know what their teachers value they seek to comply. Language is no exception. Look at some of the metaphors these youngsters created for colors, modeling their poetry after Mary O'Neill's poems in *Hailstones and Halibut Bones*:

> *Yellow is a hummingbird's*
> *song . . .*

> *Purple is a muffled sneeze . . .*

White is Edelweiss
  sprinkled with dew
and the sweet scent of flower.

Original metaphors bring vividness and freshness to poetry and to writing in general.

PETER POET'S ALL-TIME FAMOUS BALANCING ACT

Many poems demonstrate a "parallel grammatical structure" (better known to my classes as "Peter Poet's All-Time Famous Balancing Act"), in which a poet breaks a line into two parts that relate to one another, or in which two lines can relate to one another. For example, the first part of a line or the first of two lines may state something, and the second part or the following line may reinforce the same thing but in different words.

Speak gently, Spring,
  and make no sudden sound;

Each part in a sense balances and restates the other. Lew Sarett uses this technique in his poem, "Four Little Foxes."

Walk softly, March,
  forbear the bitter blow;

Kids need to discover the balance within a poem to appreciate it fully. By looking for "Peter Poet's All-Time Famous Balancing Act," youngsters can direct their attention to noticing part of the poet's craft. Taking the opening stanzas of a poem like "All Things Bright and Beautiful," I help kids discover the balance in the poet's lines:

All things bright and beautiful,
  All creatures great and small,
All things wise and wonderful,
  The Lord God made them all.

Each little flower that opens,
  Each little bird that sings,
He made their glowing colors,
  He made their tiny wings.

(CECIL FRANCES ALEXANDER, "All Things Bright and Beautiful")

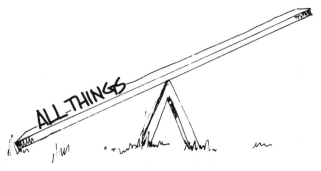

Figure 3–9

I might draw a picture like Figure 3–9 and ask the kids, "What do we need to balance my picture?"

The class would add the words "bright and beautiful." Using our hands like a balance, we see that the two parts work together.

Good!
How about the next lines?
What balance can you find?

Soon the children discover other parallels in the poem (see Figures 3–10 and 3–11).

By tuning their ears to the balances within a poem, children learn how poetry works. By applying their own insights they can shake hands with a poet by modeling their own poetry after hers. Eleanor Farjeon wrote a beautiful little poem entitled "Poetry" in which she created metaphorical balances. In it she states that poetry is "not the sky, but the light in the sky; not the sea, but the sound of the

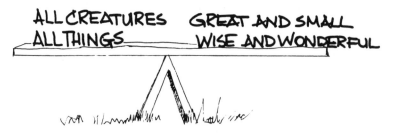

Figure 3–10

EACH LITTLE FLOWER   THAT OPENS
EACH LITTLE BIRD   THAT SINGS

Figure 3-11

sea." Children, once they sense these balances, can create their own.

Here are lines modeled after Farjeon's poem that were created by youngsters from some of my classes:

Not a tear, but the shape of a tear.

Not the wind, but the force of the wind.

Not a song, but the rhythm of a song.

Understanding the balance or balances created in a poem gives young writers a form for their own poetic visions.

HEY, THAT SOUNDED LIKE POETRY!

Most of us have at some time sat, totally untrained, and poked at a piano. A key here, another one there, then a bunch of keys. More than likely what we produced was horrendous. But if our ears could bear it and we stayed at it long enough, there was a chance that by sheer, serendipitous luck, somewhere along the line we would hit upon a series of notes, maybe even a chord, that didn't pierce our eardrums. For some reason those random notes sounded almost like music.

You wouldn't have to be a trained pianist to know that those notes sounded . . . well, right together. Your ear would simply tell you.

The poet works much in the same way except that while he pokes around with words he is fully aware of what he eventually wants. He strives to find just the right word in just the right arrangement, with just the right image, making just the right line and in just the right structure. He wants the line that serves his poetic intention most meaningfully. In essence, he wants the perfect word performance.

When I write, as is my habit, I often listen to classical music. Even today as I write this section with Pachelbel's "Kanon" playing in the background, I'm struck by the fact that no other musical note in the whole universe of notes could possibly, to my mind, be substituted for any note of what I'm hearing. Nor could any infinitesimal part of a second be added or shaved from any pause or hesitation in the whole piece. Why? My ears tell me so! It's just right. This same sense of *just right* is what poets strive for in their work.

The process of the poet is like yours at the piano, picking at the keys until your ear says, "Hey, that sounded like music!" It's reported that Dylan Thomas kept only two lines of poetry a day out of probably hundreds of scribbled phrases and lines. One can only imagine ruddy-faced Dylan, cigarette crossing his chin, saying, "Hey,, that sounded like poetry!"

Of all the ideas I try to get across to children about poetry, the *just right* word, *just right* image, *just right* rhythm, *just right* metaphor is the hardest. I try to help children understand that the poet strives as hard as an Olympic athlete to perfect what he does. I want them to understand that a line of poetry is like a baseball hit: a good poetic line is a good, safe, base hit, a memorable image a double—but the line of poetry that will last and last is a home run. Everything works perfectly—the stance, the pitch, the grip, the swing, and the contact. And the ball lands in the grandstands.

POETIC BREATH—WORDS
CHOREOGRAPHED IN SOUND

The key to having children understand the "grand slam hit effect" in poetry is that they read poetry well. Reading poetry well is dependent on coming to hear its "poetic breaths." The "poetic breath" (as I refer to it) is the grouping of words into a phrase or line that is meaningful to the ear and to our capacity to understand. I call this grouping a breath because a breath is a continuous flow of air uninterrupted by a pause. Take, for example, the beginning lines of Henry Wadsworth Longfellow's "Paul Revere's Ride":

Listen, my children, and you shall hear
Of the midnight ride of Paul Revere,

On the eighteenth of April, in Seventy-five;
Hardly a man is now alive
Who remembers that famous day and year.

Reading it well would not be accomplished by reading it like the uniform donging of a grandfather clock:

Listen (pause*) my* (pause*) chil* (pause*) dren* (pause*)
   and (pause*) you* . . .

I've actually heard teachers read this way to their classes. Spoken words have a natural linguistic phrasing, and in poetry phrasing is imperative. Words in poems are not solo dancers, performing in isolation on the stage, but an ensemble of dancers working together, choreographing the whole poem.

Listen my children, (healthy pause)
and you shall hear (pause)
Of the midnight ride (pause)
of Paul Revere, (pause)
On the eighteenth (slight pause)
of April, (pause)
in Seventy-five (pause) . . .

Each of the groups of words represents a "poetic breath," which makes the poem sound like spoken language to our ears. We can hear the words of a poem, in its correct poetic breaths, as a voice speaking in our heads.

Not all uses of language rely as heavily as poetry on linguistic breaths to enable comprehension. I suspect that newspaper articles, particularly those written down to accommodate youngsters in the classroom, can be understood without sensing linguistic breaths. Sadly, the same can be said of some of the stories included in many basals. Kids often read with just their eyes, not searching for the linguistic structuring of the writing—more like fishing for information with their eyes. During the discussion afterwards they keep reeling up possible answers until their teacher tells them they have caught the right one.

To read poetry, to read it fluidly and with meaningful expression, children must intuitively break the wording into poetic breaths.

Once again, only the *Sounds of Language* reading series stresses the concept of poetic breaths as one of its fundamental skills of reading. The series refers to what I term "poetic breaths" as "chunks of meaning." The book has its readers "cluster words into the sound of sense."

Many of its stories are in clusters of words, much like the grouping I did for the Longfellow poem. The books in the series ignore the traditional printing method of starting-at-the-left-margin-proceed-with-a-row-of-words-until-you-reach-the-right-margin. These books gear both the eye and the ear to the natural phrasing of language. I refer you to the delightful conversation between Bill Martin Jr, and the cantankerous ghost, Noodles, in the section called "Language Works in Chunks of Meaning." Bill explains to Noodles:

Language begins in the head
and always works in chunks . . .
chunks of meaning . . .
words are held together
by the sound of sense.
(Martin and Brogan 1972, 68–69)

Trust your ears

If there was one phrase other than a very patronizing, "Class, let's please be quiet," that I used again and again during a school year, it must have been, "Trust your ears." Trusting our ears allows us to find a poem's beauty and meaning. But ears, like eyes and fingers, must be trained—or, better expressed—be "lovingly exposed."

I don't believe I could expect students who have never heard the pulsating, tightly knit rhythm of a ballad to be able on their own to discover that same cadence. However, after they have heard many well-read ballads, I see students relying on their ears to help them read a ballad successfully.

Poetry is learned as much through the ear as through the reading eye. Much of what is learned through the ear must be modeled from another's voice. Children listen to their parents. They imitate their expressions and phraseology in their own speaking voices. As a result, they sound like their parents. I suspect a good many teachers could match parents and children by only listening to them speak.

The same is true when children learn to read poetry; they listen to poetry being read, then imitate that voice in their own reading. I always remember a friend who left her young daughter with her husband's parents while she worked during the day. Now, my friend had a nice Midwest accent (or lack of accent, depending on where you're from), and her husband's parents were from the deep South. As a result, her daughter's everyday talk was typical Great Plains. But, come time to recite a nursery rhyme she'd learned from Grandma, that girl's voice came straight from Dixie!

But accents are only part of what children imitate. They also imitate the phrasing of the words. The young child's mind stores the phraseology of a well-read poem, and that is as much a gift as the poem itself. Kids whose ears are tuned to language through a teacher's voice come to want to hear that voice. Whenever I was absent from school and needed a substitute, my class preferred that the substitute not continue reading whatever I happened to be reading to them at the time. They had come to associate my voice and my vocal phrasing with the particular book.

With younger children I have always read poetry as part of my daily story time. Not just simple poems to satisfy the seasonal changes—a "quickie" October poem for the first day of October— but a variety of poems: story poems, ballads, nonsense poems, long poems, short poems. All kinds of poems. And, yes, even some poems they wouldn't understand. We forget that there is satisfaction simply in listening, even if a poem is strange to the listener's ear.

Training their ears to hear

On occasion I'd mimeograph a poem and, after reading it a couple of times, I'd pass out copies.

Kids, listen with your ears and follow with your eyes, and let's see how many can spot exactly where I take a breath.

After I read the poem again, we'd highlight in different colors the words I'd grouped together. Then we'd read the poem in unison.

Another activity I have used to help younger kids train their ears and discover the "poetic breaths" of a poem is to leave copies of poems out with scissors and long, one-inch strips of unlined paper. The kids take one of the poems and break it into its poetic breaths (one strip of paper for each breath) to make a hanging mobile. I use one of my own poems to demonstrate how to do it (see Figure 3–12).

Figure 3–12

THE GIFT

If I were to
give to you
a gift, so true,

Then, my friend,
I would give
you to you.

And you too
could celebrate in
the gift of you.

And I, the visions
of the yous you're to become.

With older kids, I have them search on their own for a poem's poetic breath. Working with David Wagoner's "Staying Alive," I introduce the poem by asking them to imagine that they are lost in the wilderness, completely separated from their group. "What would you do?" I ask them. "Here's the beginning of a poem with all the answers."

Staying alive in the woods is a matter of calming down
At first and deciding whether to wait for rescue,
Trusting to others,
Or simply to start walking and walking in one direction
Till you come out—or something happens to stop you.
By far the safer choice
Is to settle down where you are, and try to make a living
Off the land, camping near water, away from shadows . . .

(DAVID WAGONER, "Staying Alive")

"Before you start, could someone read the poem?" Being completely fooled by the poem's line structure (as I'm sure many of you were), someone bravely reads. A hodgepodge of seemingly disconnected thoughts comes out. I apologize for tricking the person and tell the group to "trust their ears" and "find the poetic breaths." The poem will make sense. They work and, in between moans and groans, verbal signs of slight recognition emerge. "Use your ears. They'll bring meaning to the piece," I encourage.

Soon someone breaks the deadlock. Comprehensible meaning does exist in the poem. Now somebody reads:

Staying alive in the woods/
is a matter/
of calming down at first/
and deciding whether to wait for rescue/
trusting to others/
or simply to start walking/
and walking in one direction/
till you come out/
or something happens to stop you. /
By far/
the safer choice /
is to settle down where you are /
and try to make a living off the land /
camping near water/
away from shadows/. .

The poetic breaths give meaning to the poem. We go on to discuss the entire poem, argue over parts, and eventually better understand what the poem is trying to do.

As I have done with the above poem, I often have the class draw slashes between the phrases of a new poem to break it into its poetic breaths. This guides the mind's listening ear to "hear" the poem as it is read. It helps the individual poem to become meaningful and clarifies the nature of poetry in general.

SO MUCH ALIKE, BUT, OH, SO DIFFERENT

Any accomplished guitarist knows that it's not the simple stroke of his thumb across the strings of the guitar that determines the musical quality of his music. Along with the stroke is the chord and how his fingers press the strings at the neck of the guitar. In addition, the melodic quality of that one chord is its relationship to the other chords, notes, and musical movements within the piece. Likewise the beat, or rhythm, of the piece cannot be singled out but needs to be seen in relation to the rest of the music.

What is the point of all this? Very simply that the success of a poem, like the guitarist's music, is a concerted effort of all the poetic techniques used within a poem. It is the ensemble of all the different word performances working together. Just as the enjoyment of a circus doesn't come from only viewing individual performances one at a time, but rather from the festive nature of everything going on at once, so it is, too, with the enjoyment of poetry. Understanding a poem comes not from focusing on singled-out elements, but seeing all the elements as they orchestrate the purpose or intent of the poem. The satisfaction found in poetry is found in its "wholeness."

The word choices, rhythm, rhyme, imagery, metaphors, and visual design are only the tools of the poet. Her purpose and artistic vision use these tools. One cannot simply use, say, rhyme, and be convinced he has written poetry. If that were the case, a formula could be developed and anyone with an adequate vocabulary who is able to follow the formula could write poetry. Poetry is and always will be an art. And art determines itself. Artists use what is available to them. They create from their own inner need. That's what makes the teaching of poetry so challenging and exciting. Each poem presents itself differently and introduces its own vast array of teaching possibilities. Each poem is like a new child in your classroom— so very much like the rest of your class, but, oh, so unique. Getting to know him and what makes him tick—like each new poem you teach—is half the fun.

PART II
TEACHING POETRY

PROBLEMS IN
THE TEACHING OF POETRY
. . . a slow road to appreciation

NATURE OF THE CRITTER

Given the choice, I suspect most children (and many adults as well) would prefer an ice cream cone to a plate of raw vegetables, would choose hanging out with friends over working on a research paper, and would rather tap their toes to pop music than listen to a symphony in a stuffy concert hall. Likewise, I suspect that many kids would rather watch a television miniseries version of a novel than devote long, solitary hours to reading the novel. In the same vein, if they were up to reading, I suspect they would prefer an action-packed popular book to some more serious, perhaps inspirational, poetry. It's the nature of the human critter to want initially the quickest, most immediately satisfying experience rather than a deeper, more demanding experience.

As I write this section there's a splendid day developing just outside my study window—a day perfect for a leisurely hike up "Johnson's Trail" or even, perhaps, a bicycle ride. In all honesty I would prefer to jump into my hiking shoes or riding shorts and be gone. And while I'm being honest, there are numerous evenings that even I—the epitome of a true poetry lover—would rather slip into a "quick and dirty" television program than thumb through a new anthology of poetry.

By nature, I believe, we prefer the more immediately satisfying experiences that require little or no effort. Popular music, television, and even loafing appeal to us. Experiences such as art, classical music, academic pursuits, and, yes, poetry, require more. Intense listening, previous study, reflection, and active probing with our minds are nearly prerequisite to appreciating the arts. This inherently requires some effort. Does this effort diminish their value? Certainly not, to my mind. For as much as I would like to hike or bicycle on a beautiful, late summer day, there is still the knowledge of how rewarding it will be to see this book completed.

Learning to appreciate the finer things in life—as art, music, theater, and poetry have been called—is an acquired ability. I wasn't born with an ear for classical music. In fact, as I recall, I didn't much like it as a child. Nor was I born with a masochistic longing for academic work and a dislike of physical activity outdoors. I did not stumble by way of my childhood creek headfirst into a love of poetry. No, I was exposed to music, to the satisfaction of writing, to the wonders of poetry and art. In a sense I came to appreciate a balanced diet that included vegetables as well as ice cream.

FULLY EDUCATED INDIVIDUAL

I somehow think that we in education have forgotten that our job includes exposing our students to aspects of our culture that can make their lives more enriched. We seem to have succumbed to the side of ourselves that wants immediate gratification. Our focus seems to be not on what can enrich us but on what will make us rich—that is to say, marketable job skills. We are quick to justify a new, more relevant math or science program on the basis of one governmental report; we are quicker still to jump on any educational bandwagon at the slightest hint that our children lag behind the Japanese. Unfortunately, we are even quicker to let the arts slide. Art teachers are notoriously the first to go during school budgetary crunches. Sound instruction in art and art appreciation is replaced by crafts and activities in the regular classroom. Music programs are becoming deemphasized, while dance and theater instruction are becoming extracurricular options. It's ironic that those things which, in life's long run, can be most satisfying to our students are the first to go from our schools' curricula.

Certainly, viable and comprehensive math, reading, and writing programs are essential to public education—as is computer literacy. Even with my mistrust of some of the effects of computer mania, I must acknowledge that if it weren't for the computer and its word-processing capacity, this particular book could still be scribbled notes.

My point quite simply is that a fully educated individual has skills and knowledge beyond those necessary for his occupations. The many arts—music, dance, theater, literature, and poetry—are vital components of a fully realized life. Most importantly, appreciation of the arts is not acquired at birth. It must be learned.

THE NEGLECTED COMPONENT

Studies show that poetry is the most neglected component in the language arts curriculum and that there is a sharp decrease in the amount of time teachers spend reading and sharing poetry with their classes as students advance from the primary to the intermediate levels of elementary school. Ann Terry's research, published in her book *Children's Poetry Preferences*, suggests that over a nine-month period, twenty-five percent of the teachers in her survey read poetry to their class only nine times, while fifty percent of the teachers read it even less (Terry 1974, 41). Is it any surprise that with less and less exposure to poetry children's interest in poetry declines as they progress up the elementary school ladder?

Research also reveals that unless poetry is important to the individual teacher's own life (as was the case in my teaching career), then the teacher knows little about it and is reluctant to use it in the classroom. This research seems to reflect all that I've mentioned. Our curricular side step of poetry (as well as the other arts) has relegated it to an optional status. Uninterested teachers, then, feel no pressure to become more knowledgeable and proficient in their teaching of poetry. Consequently, they may teach it less and less, and unfortunately, may be uninspired when they do. Sadly, children who receive such weak instruction in poetry have few opportunities to hear, read, and write poetry.

We all remember how we were taught poetry—both through inspired teaching and uninspired instruction. Many times after a workshop, teachers will confide in me about how much they hated forced memorization and seemingly endless examination on nitpicking parts of some obscure poem. The whole situation is compounded by the natural tendency of older children to shy away from poetry and to prefer popular music and television.

I don't think that knowledgeable and caring teachers should be confined to shifting curricular patterns or the immediate likes and dislikes of children. The situation should challenge our creative energies. We should be inspired by the knowledge that we can pass on to our students something universally beautiful. We can help them enjoy poetry along with ice cream, pop music, and, of course, loafing. Their lives will be a bit richer as a result of our efforts.

Poetry in the reading basals—second cousin to the real stuff

I wonder if part of students' degenerating interest in poetry as they grow older comes in part from poetry's presentation in our basal series. Since so much of our reading and language instruction today comes from basal series, it is safe to assume, unless a teacher has a personal interest in poetry, that what is presented in the basal will pretty much be the extent of the poetry taught.

The typical teaching process for poetry in basals includes:

1. Read the poem aloud while the class listens.
2. Read it again, having the students follow in their books.
3. Discuss the poem.
4. Let the students read it aloud.

While not a bad process per se, it is terribly uninvolving and unimaginative. I doubt whether repeating this process with every poem in the English language would ever lead anyone to a love of poetry. Furthermore, the selection of poetry represented in the basals, I feel, is weak. Rarely were any of the poems in my basals the ones with which I could really get my kids involved. The emphasis given to poetry in our basals seems to be based on the idea that poetry is a cute and lighthearted sidekick to the real reading stuff—the stories and skill lessons.

Stories in basals have a great many motivational suggestions and discussion questions that measure not only students' literal comprehension but their understanding and appreciation of the pieces as well. Then come the "goodies"—the skill instructions to go along with the story, not to mention the workbook pages and the duplicated sheets, and finally, testing. Meanwhile the good little poem, bless its soul, is heard, discussed quickly, and read silently—then it's time to roar off to the next story.

What happens to poetry, in my observation, is one of three things. First, it is deemphasized—read, discussed, and forgotten. It may be covered in a quick two-week language arts lesson: limericks in the fourth grade, similes in the fifth. Or second, it is taught as story— new vocabulary words looked up, content read silently, and comprehension questions written out. Or third, the poems may be skipped over entirely or left to students' free-time reading. To me none of these approaches is suitable. I do understand, however, how a teacher with little training in poetry and no personal interest in it could fall into one of these traps.

Another inherent problem is the predominant attitude in the basals of "cover-the-ground-and-move-on." There is a relentless push in the pages of a basal to do all the activities associated with a selection, and then it's on-to-the-next-book-and-whatever-you-do-don't-look-back. Poetry, however, will require a slow road to appreciation, a road that loops quietly back to allow time to reconsider, to rethink. We must hear a poem many times, on different occasions, in different moods and settings to understand it fully. I'm still learning about poems that I have studied and recited for six years.

You might think about teaching poetry as taking your class on a tour through a fine arts museum. You wouldn't treat each painting identically: "Class, let's look for just a minute and we'll talk about it and you can take one last look before we go on to the next painting." You would allow time for children to look and mull over and wander about and come back to a painting. Each painting is unique and presents itself for pondering. Whether it's the painting's use of line, its color scheme, or its statement, it requires time to be considered fully. So, too, with poetry. Some poems beg to be dramatized, others illustrated. Some poems want only to be left quietly in the back pocket of one's mind, while others need to be danced to or sung. Finding ways for children to experience poetry is the task of creative teachers.

There is a need in the study of poetry to discover, experience, and retain. This need can rarely be met by the hear-talk-about-and-read-aloud sprinkling the subject receives in our basals. That approach is rather like giving a child poetry as you would a distasteful medicine . . . a little mandatory dose here, another there. Children should be exposed to poetry throughout the year, throughout the curriculum, in a variety of ways. My survival kit to accompany a basal in your poetry program would include the following suggestions:

- *Don't* allow poetry to be a second cousin to the other language selections in the book.
- *Expand*, enhance, redirect, and enrich the suggested activities included in the teacher's guide so that your students can more fully experience the poem and appreciate its poetic craftsmanship.
- *Bring* additional poetry into all areas of your curriculum. Avoid teaching poetry as an isolated language arts unit. Share poems about insects in science units or poems about famous Americans throughout social studies.
- *Don't* shy away from more difficult or complex poetry. Try it— if it fails you have learned something, if it works you have given something.
- *Finally*, along with your students, develop and sensitize your own ear to good poetry.

The reader might note that at the end of this book I have included not only a listing of individual poems and poetry anthologies I have found useful, but also a sampling of poetry activities that could be included in a learning center. I hope that these sources and activities will give you a place to start in bringing poetry to life in your classroom.

A hidden valley

A friend of mine and his wife are avid cross-country skiers, having many years ago retired their downhill skiing gear. For those of you unfamiliar with the differences between the two types of skiing, let me explain briefly. Downhill skiing is an exceedingly fast sport. The bumps and mogols on the hill provide an exhilarating experience. The combined sensations of speed, near loss of control, and short flights off the snow's surface are immediately thrilling.

Cross-country skiing, on the other hand, is a slower-paced activity—a rhythmic, gliding experience. In many cases it's quiet and solitary, perhaps more reflective in nature. A cross-country skier spends time with his own thoughts. The rewards in cross-country skiing many times revolve around a snow picnic, or finding a hidden snow valley or abandoned cabin.

My friends have a young son and would like him to come to enjoy cross-country skiing as they do. The son, however, is old enough to join his friends and go up to the downhill areas. It's only natural that he, for now, prefers the speed and excitement of downhill skiing as opposed to the slow-paced, cross-country outings of the family. As with many young people, his fearless and agile body responds to the thrills found in downhill skiing.

Marvelously, though, his parents can understand this and they are patiently allowing him to do both. They don't want to force cross-country skiing on him but would like him to come to appreciate both activities. So they make their cross-country outings as fun as possible and carefully try to expose him to the quieter, slower-paced pleasure to be found in cross-country skiing, while still allowing him to enjoy the thrills of downhill skiing. They are comfortable knowing that someday he'll probably come to see its joys as they do.

In my friends' situation I see a perfect parallel to the teaching of poetry. Downhill skiing with its immediate sensation of speed and thrill is sort of like popular music and television, fast-paced and quickly gratifying. Poetry is much slower-paced and its rewards, like the hidden valley, take time and effort to reach. I don't expect kids, particularly older kids, to ignore their natural tendencies and immediately love all the poetry I teach. My position as a teacher is like my friends' with their son. I understand the likes and dislikes of youngsters, so I make my poetry presentations as exciting as I can. I'm also patient enough to give kids the time they need to learn to appreciate poetry. I try not to force too much, too soon. Kids also need their music and television. Any dieter knows that a steady diet of bland greens and carrots can make one miserable. We need our hits of ice cream.

Nurturing

In the same way that my friends couldn't throw a pair of cross-country skis at their son and expect him automatically to enjoy and appreciate what they had come to enjoy in cross-country touring, we can't simply slap our favorite poem on the kids' desks and expect them to devour it like chocolate cake. More than likely, we have come to love that particular poem because of our life experiences. Kids without similar experiences might not respond the same way we do. We need to focus our sights on helping youngsters grow comfortably into poetry.

An aesthetic response can *only* be nurtured. To nurture poetry, like most arts, requires that we carefully expose children to the language of poetry over a long period of time. In order for my students to begin to appreciate my wonderful collection of winter poems, I must be showing them poetry in early fall.

I'm confident that by carefully exposing my class to a series of poems and sharing my enthusiasm, their sensitivity to poetry will emerge. Will every single student become an avid poetry reader? More than likely, no. Some students this year. Some more, perhaps, a few years down the road. Some maybe never. But my task is to strive toward poetic appreciation in my class—not to be disillusioned when everyone is not tearing down the library walls for copies of Chaucer's *Canterbury Tales*. Although my father taught me to catch a baseball, I don't believe he's disillusioned that I don't play for the Yankees. Much the same with poetry. Poetry taught creatively and understandingly can create a situation in which children make it their own, much like love, in their own way and in their own time.

Making it your own

I wonder if the waning interest in poetry is limited solely to growing youngsters. A while back I was speaking before a group of teachers at a conference and began by asking the audience how many of them had read the newspaper that morning. A fair percentage of hands went up. I then asked how many had read a magazine in the last week. Again a high percentage. How about a novel in the last three or four months? A limited number of hands went up. Some professional material? An overwhelming number of hands were in the air. But when I asked how many had read or reread some poetry not associated with their teaching responsibilities, barely a handful responded.

Poetry simply isn't read much these days. Not long ago I ran into a woman who was a 1930 graduate of the Northeastern School of Oral Interpretation and had made a living back then by reading and reciting poetry as a one-woman show. She told me how, when she was performing in the 1940s and 1950s, people were well-read in poetry and familiar with any of the pieces she did. "Any educated person at that time," she said, "was well versed in literature and poetry."

Much has changed since then and principally, I feel, through the invention of the television. Poetry simply isn't as popular with large numbers of people as it once was, whether teachers or others. Yet it never fails that after one of my workshops (which, as I have mentioned, include a good deal of poetry recitation), someone comes to me bursting with enthusiasm for a poem I have recited, which he had long forgotten. It's almost as if he is seeing a long-lost friend. "I remember reading that poem as a child and loving it." The poetry I shared opened a window that had been stuck from years and layers of paint. The listeners often ask:

"Do you read . . . ?"

"Have you heard . . . ?"

"Will you recite . . . ?"

Although this recollection and the desire to hear more poetry is terribly exciting and flattering to me, it is also evidence that poetry is still close to many hearts—perhaps stuffed in the back closet of the mind, cluttered with many other things, but still as moving and important as it was the day it was first heard.

If I had my way, a teacher unable to share at least ten poems with kids would not be allowed in a classroom. Perhaps the first step good teachers need to make in teaching poetry to children is to reactivate their own poetic reservoir and make some special poems their own.

Donna E. Norton's book *Through the Eyes of a Child* lists eight activities designed for reactivating an adult appreciation of poetry: activities such as looking through an anthology of poetry and finding the elements of poetry—rhyme, alliteration, assonance, imagery and metaphor—or reading a selection of humorous poetry by Edward Lear or Lewis Carroll (Norton 1983, 346). A suggestion I would add to this list is that you search high and low for those poems that moved you as a youngster and reread them.

One of the first requirements of the poetry class I offer to teachers is that each one of them find a special, moving poem remembered from childhood. I have them try to recall the situation of the poem. Who taught it to them? What book was it from? What do they remember of how they felt? I always look forward to the class period when they share these recollections. One might bring a tattered, treasured old copy of Robert Louis Stevenson's poetry, a book handed down through a family for years. Another might recall the wrinkled old cheeks of the grandfather who recited, from memory, ballads of Robert Service. One student told how, as a little girl, she went to bed every night with her mother singing a poem over and over, each time softer, until she fell asleep. Tapping into your own poetic memories is a rewarding way in which to set the stage for poetry instruction in your classroom.

By fostering your own appreciation of poetry, you greatly enhance your ability to foster a love or appreciation in others. If we know anything about teaching it is that teachers' likes and dislikes are contagious. We should exploit this. I always explained straight-faced to my big, sophisticated fifth graders that they would be in a fair amount of trouble if they could not abide by the school rules, but if anyone, at any time, under any circumstances, said anything bad about Robert Frost . . . well, we're talking about immediate suspension from school. Needless to say, my kids loved old Bob Frost.

One of the most charming books of poetry for younger students I've come upon is the late John Ciardi's *You Read to Me, I'll Read to You.* If you've not seen this book, it is a collection of his poetry printed in alternating blue and black ink. The parent or adult reads the ones printed in blue to the child, and the child then reads the ones in black. The marvelous thing about the book, of course, is the child in her parent's lap hearing and reading poetry.

In my classrooms I have always had shelves of poetry books, ranging from adult to juvenile poetry. On occasion we'd have a "favorite poem read-athon." Everyone read or recited one favorite poem. Many times my classes heard poetry that had no more chance of ending up in their basal than did Sanskrit. I was well aware of the fact that they might not completely understand a poem, but that gave me something to talk about afterwards with them, and I was modeling—modeling an adult with a good book of poetry—which might have been my most potent and lasting moment of teaching.

GETTING THROUGH THE POETICS
TO THE POEM

The problem many kids in upper and middle grades have with poetry is that the juvenile rhymes and jingles they enjoyed a few years before are no longer satisfying to their growing egos. "Baby stuff!" they say. Their minds crave deeper, more sophisticated experiences and what they know of poetry doesn't appear to satisfy that side of them. Poetry, in effect, has gotten a bad reputation with many older kids. It doesn't have a good, mind-riveting story, nor does it have any information that interests them. So why read it?

However, much of the finest poetry and that which is the easiest to use with older kids is in the form of story poems. Research such as Ann Terry's on the likes and dislikes of children shows that they prefer poems that tell stories and have a humorous element. William Cole has two wonderful collections of story poems, *A Poet's Tale*

Figure 4–1

and *Story Poems*, that should be part of any teacher's resources. Think of the story poems you learned while growing up. Along with the classic "The Cremation of Sam McGee," how about Longfellow's "Hiawatha" and "Paul Revere's Ride" or Noyes's "The Highwayman" or Riley's "The Raggedy Man" or Browning's "Pied Piper" or Poe's "The Raven"? The list could go on and on.

One of the best collections of stories I know is Iona and Peter Opie's *The Oxford Book of Narrative Verse*, but I'll wager that you'd recognize only a couple of them. Why? Because they're written in poetry and we, like our students, have to work to get through the poetics to the story. I have helped my young readers of story poems to see the story embedded within the poetics through the use of a "Story Sequence" sheet. An example, reduced in size from those I have used in my classes, is shown in Figure 4–1. Taking one story poem from the many collections, students read it and, while reading, outline the chain of events in the boxes. After they have discovered the story—simply, what happened— they can answer a series of questions more typically used with stories:

- Who are the characters?
- What is the setting?
- What problem or conflict exists in the story?
- How is that conflict or problem resolved?
- What was the climax of the story?

From this point, students have a handle on the story and are free to examine the poetics. They may find and store some of the poet's "star" words and their favorite images in their poetry notebooks. A dramatic reading may be in order. Many other possibilities can surface when students discover that the poem was simply a good story written in poetic language.

It might be interesting to note that much early poetry actually consisted of story poems created by bards and troubadours celebrating the feats and accomplishments of kings and warriors. Do you recall reading *Beowulf* or Homer's *Iliad* or *Odyssey*? In fact, in some early cultures it was believed that a person lived on in the memory of the people as long as they talked about him and recounted his feats. What king or warrior wouldn't want a ballad written about him so that following generations could keep him alive for eternity?

Getting to the content

A while back I was asked to be the breakfast speaker at a "Newspaper in Education" conference. Sponsored by the local newspaper, the conference was, of course, to promote the use of newspapers in the classroom. When my wife heard that I was to speak, she asked in a charmingly sarcastic tone tolerated only within the bounds of marriage, "Well, how are you going to use *poetry* with the newspaper?"

The more I thought about it, the more I realized that much poetry is a story about an event, fictional or actual, and that newspaper articles are also stories about events. They are simply written in different styles. So why couldn't the immediacy—the this-is-real-and-it's-happening-now effect—of the newspaper be used to teach poetry? Couldn't the newspaper help a student get through a poem's poetics to the story?

Grabbing my trustworthy collection of Robert Service poems, I asked myself, "What if a *Gazette* reporter had covered the same event that Service has written about? How would the reporter write about it?" So I became the reporter. Imagine that you and your class open the morning newspaper to these lines.

DOUBLE MURDER IN LOCAL SALOON INVESTIGATED

ESTER, ALASKA (NIE)—Police were called to the Malamute Saloon after an apparent double murder late last night. The Malamute, a popular "watering hole" for the men who pan the area's gold, is no stranger to disturbances. It has been frequented by such characters as "One-Eyed Mike," "Hard-Luck Henry," and "Gum-Boot Ben." But this is the first time that two men were apparently killed by each other's guns.

At this time, police are only saying that Daniel McGrew (better-known around these parts as Dangerous Dan McGrew) and an as yet unidentified man are both dead. McGrew received multiple gunshot wounds to the head while the unidentified man was killed by a bullet that pierced his heart.

Eyewitnesses say that last night began much like any night at the Malamute with an abundance of music, whiskey, and poker. And then the stranger arrived. McGrew was reportedly playing cards by himself at the back of the bar. He was accompanied by his lady-friend (known as Lou). Sometime around midnight the stranger appeared. According to witnesses, the stranger seemed to be "half dead" as he ordered drinks for the whole house. "He had a 'poke' [a gold dust pouch worn by miners and strung to their belts] full of gold dust like we never seen in these parts," stated one patron who was at the scene.

For some unexplained reason, the stranger then began playing the piano and tension built up between McGrew and the stranger although no words were exchanged between the men. Some witnesses report that Lou (McGrew's lady) couldn't keep her eyes off the stranger, as if they had known each other before.

Malamute bartender Pete Henry reported that he was serving McGrew a drink when he observed McGrew engaged in an activity he had never seen him perform at a poker table. According to Henry, McGrew made a "spread misere" [a poker tactic in which the player spreads his cards out face up, obviously intending to lose]. "Why Dan did that I'll never know," stated Henry, "but moments later the stranger shouted at McGrew and the gunfight began."

For now, all the police seem to know is that two men are
dead and that money is missing from one of them.

Following the reading of the article, my class discussed the basic
who, where, what, and *why* of the event.

- Who is the article about?
- Tell as much as you can about the article's characters.
- What happened?
- Where did it happen?
- Why do you think it happened?

We also discussed unfamiliar vocabulary ("poke of dust" and
"spread misere"). Now the class knew the storyline and was familiar
with the vocabulary, so they were given a copy of Robert Service's
"The Shooting of Dan McGrew." In addition, I made a tape of the
poem available. The students were able to hear and appreciate the
poem's story and safely negotiated the maze of the poetics.

An approach such as this takes into account what we know about
reading and the processes that go on in individuals while they read.
Frank Smith, in his very fine book, *Reading Without Nonsense,*
talks about the two kinds of information that one must use in order
to read. He distinguishes between "visual information," or clues
that are picked up with the eye solely from the printed page, and
"nonvisual information" that is already stored in our minds, such
as an understanding of relevant language, a familiarity with the
subject at hand, and a general ability in reading. Smith contends
that there is a reciprocal relationship between these types of information in the act of reading:

The more nonvisual information you have when you read,
the less visual information you need.

The less nonvisual information you have when you read,
the more visual information you need.
(Smith 1985, 14)

Readers like our students, who are not familiar with the language
of poetry, therefore need more nonvisual information to help them
grasp a poem. They simply can't rely solely on the print or visual
information. It baffles them. So we must "prime the pump" and
supply them with an adequate amount of nonvisual information.
The process I described with Robert Service's "The Shooting of Dan

McGrew" gives students the necessary nonvisual information to arrive at a comfortable point in understanding the content of the poem, a point they might not otherwise have been able to reach. I invite my readers to read Frank Smith's texts, particularly *Reading Without Nonsense*, for a deeper and assuredly better understanding of this idea.

Again drawing on these principles, I used a newspaper format to create a "grabber" or "hook" for another of Service's poems. I wanted students to read with a haunting question lingering on their minds.

INVESTIGATORS PUZZLED

LONDON, ENGLAND (NIE)—Local police are puzzled about the disappearance of a soon-to-be-published poet, gold miner, and vagabond. Robert W. Service, who grew up near Liverpool and spent his childhood in Glasgow, has long been noted for his characteristic wanderlust. His travels have reportedly led him throughout Turkey, Mexico, Canada, and Alaska. It was in Alaska during the Gold Rush that he adopted the lifestyle of a "sourdough," a rugged, seasoned gold miner. He recently returned to London in order to oversee the printing of his ballads, which will soon be published in his first collection of poetry, entitled *Songs of the Sourdough*.

According to friends of the poet, Service acquired a fortune in Alaska and it was also in Alaska that he wrote his poems, transforming the stories and yarns he heard into ballads and songs.

Police are concerned because Service returned to London a rich man, due to profits acquired from mining gold in the wilds of Alaska. It has been reported that Service has squandered much of his money, drinking champagne with every meal and gambling away his money as if in a hurry to be rid of it. Authorities are concerned because Service seems to have left London with no apparent reason or explanation.

In an attempt to understand the disappearance, friends of Service recount stories of the poet's life in Alaska. Apparently, the environment there could be likened to that of hell. "Famine and scurvy were rampant and death an everyday occurrence," one friend recalled hearing Service comment. Another acquaintance of the poet stated that Service has said "goodbye to the hell of Alaska."

The only clue police have is an uncompleted poem found scribbled on the back of a menu. Its meaning, at this time, is not understood.

"I wanted the gold and I got it—
  Came out with a fortune last fall—
Yet somehow life's not what I thought it
  And somehow the gold isn't all."

The questions remain: Where did Robert W. Service go and, more importantly, why?

Again, after the article questions arise.

• What happened?
• Where did it happen?
• Why is it newsworthy?
• What do we know about the life of Service from the article?

Finally:

• Where did he go?
• WHY?

The students are now set for "The Spell of the Yukon." By presenting the poem in the way I did, I helped the students bring meaning to a piece of writing as only a story can. And again, as in the Dan McGrew piece, I used the article to supply the students with a great deal of "nonvisual information" about Robert Service and the setting in which he wrote.

Use of prediction

I'd like to offer one last example of how to help young readers get through the poetics to the content of the poem, again through the newspaper format and using what I know of Frank Smith's invaluable research. Smith boldly states that "comprehension depends on prediction." Comprehension, Smith says, occurs when the reader's predictions hold no more "unanswered questions" (Smith 1985, 72). The important thing is that the reader's questions are conceived prior to or during the act of reading. The more typical way teachers use questions is *after* the reading act and for evaluation. More typical, also, is that the questions are the teachers' questions. However, if the reader goes into the reading of a poem seeking confirmation or rejection of his own predictions, then his comprehension is enhanced.

I have youngsters design their own questions and conceive their own predictions before they read some poems. They work in twos, and I give each pair a short article, such as the one below that introduces Edna St. Vincent Millay's "Ballad of the Harp Weaver."

WOMAN DIES WEAVING ON A HARP?

CAMDEN, MAINE (NIE)—Police were summoned to a small cottage early this morning by a small boy, who from all appearances was nearly starving to death. The boy reportedly woke to find his mother frozen to death next to their harp in the house. What confuses the police, at this point, is that although there was neither food nor supplies in the house, next to the dead woman were piles of perfectly woven clothes—"fit for a king and exactly the boy's size," officers have reported. The only explanation the boy has offered is that his mother wove them on their harp last night before she died.

The group reads the article and writes down as many questions as naturally occur to them:

- Where did the clothes come from?
- Why did the mother freeze but not the boy?
- Were the clothes really woven on a harp?

And so on.

Then they compare each other's questions and they guess and create their own answers. They now can read or listen to a recording of the poem in anticipation of the answers to their own questions and predictions.

I hope these examples using the newspaper format demonstrate ways in which poetry can be presented so that students aren't forced to flounder with something with which they have little acquaintance and which offers little purpose to their reading.

Think how many other poems that kids can't seem to "get into" could be presented in like manner. Also, the youngsters could reverse the process and write articles about other poems themselves. Younger students could design headlines that capture the content of shorter poems:

- BROTHER AUCTIONS YOUNGER SISTER
(Shel Silverstein, "For Sale")

- CHILDREN REPORT SEEING BALLOONMAN AGAIN
(e e cummings, "In Just")
- LOBSTERS DANCING? CRABS PLAYING THE FIDDLE?
(Frederick J. Forster, "The Lobster and the Fiddler Crab")
- NEW DISEASE APPEARS
(Stacy Jo Crossen and Natalie Anne Covell, "Wiggly Giggles")

The possibilities are left to the creative energies of the teacher.

In addition, I refer my readers to the activities in the Resources section of this book, which I have designed to include prediction techniques and creative ways of supplying "nonvisual information."

FINALLY...

If the nature of poetry is different from that of ordinary prose, and if consequently, the problems children experience with poetry are different from ordinary reading problems, isn't it to be expected that the teaching of poetry must be different also? Poetry's slow road to appreciation requires that we expand beyond our ordinary ways of doing things and courageously and patiently lead our students through experiences with poetry that are as exciting as possible. We need to realize that how we present poetry to children will in the end affect their impressions of poetry more than will the individual poem or poems themselves.

The next two sections will examine how poetry can be taught— how I've come to teach it over the years. Much of what I present in these sections comes from a battered metal filing cabinet where, through the years, I have thrown poetry assignments, written ideas, notes, and exercises. I hope my housecleaning gives you much to work with in your classroom.

THE READING OF POETRY

*. . . coming together of the
ear, eye, and tongue*

In the previous sections I've established that poetry is by its nature a type of writing different from prose. It looks different on the page. It sounds different to our ears. It uses words in different ways and ultimately gives us a different kind of reading experience. Shouldn't we then expect that the way we approach the reading of a poem will also be different?

PREREQUISITE OF OPENNESS

To read a poem well, there is a prerequisite of "openness." The reader must be attentive to the meanings of the words as they appear on the page; these in turn will conjure up images and feelings that also require attention. A reader of poetry needs to filter her reading through her imagination in order to be able to release her mind to unrestrained responses to the poem. How does the poetry make her feel? What visual images occur in her mind? What subtle associations do parts of the poem bring to her attention? What connections spring up between lines in the poem and experiences in her life?

I've always made it a point to let kids know that I read poetry "wide-eyed and open" and in some cases am just beginning to fully appreciate certain poems. I explore new poems like an unfamiliar country, looking for the treasures the land might hold for me. Naoshi Koriyana's poem "Unfolding Bud" expresses how a poem can be opened up to reveal such treasures.

One is amazed
By a water-lily bud
Unfolding
With each passing day,
Taking on a richer color
And new dimensions.

One is not amazed,
At a first glance,
By a poem,
Which is as tight-closed
as a tiny bud.

Yet one is surprised
To see the poem
Gradually unfolding,
Revealing its rich inner self
As one reads it
Again
And over again.

While I may read a good novel stretched out on my couch, my trusty coffee cup never out of reach, I find that I need to be sitting up, fully alert, to read more difficult poetry. I also find that I need to put the poems down and return to them later in a different mind and compare the different sensations and interpretations I get with each different reading.

Comprehension-question-syndrome

The "openness" that is required in reading poetry is blocked by some of our reading instruction practices. Kids often get locked into what I call a "comprehension-question-syndrome." They have followed a reading class tradition for years: read silently, answer questions, read orally, write out answers to questions. We have conditioned them to read not with a wide-open receptiveness to what the reading experience might bring to them, but instead locked in a "finding-the-answer" gear. Their minds don't sit back and just let the sound of the language linger, as when they listen to music; rather they are imprisoned in an I-want-to-read-this-just-once-and-not-have-to-go-back-to-find-the-answers attitude.

Coming to a poem, particularly a more mature poem, with this type of conditioning simply blows them away. "How in tarnation can I find answers in this gibberish? It doesn't even make sense."

When you read a poem, you must first back off from finding its meaning or answering its questions and just listen to it. Kids find it hard to believe that you can enjoy a poem even before you understand it, that you can enjoy its unique sounds, its images, its rhythm and beat.

A poem I am presently coming to know is Dylan Thomas's "Fern Hill." I can't honestly tell you much about its meaning at this time. I have some intuitive "flashes" as to what it's up to, but nothing concrete. If made to answer the perfunctory five comprehension questions, I would no doubt fail miserably. I simply love, for now, the sound of the words. They seem to fly from my tongue like a wild sparrow and into my ears like a mysterious symphony piece.

I remember a teacher friend of mine who used to staple an obscure Gary Snyder poem to the ceiling of his second-grade classroom and on occasion glance up and read it aloud. The second graders, of course, hadn't the faintest idea what the poem meant, and he offered no explanation. He would see them looking up at it now and then, and eventually they began to speculate as to its possible meaning. I can just hear him saying to them, "You know, you may be right—I don't know—but doesn't it just 'sound' neat up there on the ceiling?"

A poetry reader needs to use more than just his reading/decoding eyes. He needs to activate his ears, or as e e cummings said so well, "the ears of my ears." He needs to hear the poetry spoken in his head. He needs to close his eyes and just listen—visualizing (as his mind will if he lets it)—and feel the ebb and flow of the words as they come to life in his mind.

Seeing the poem

Along with training her ears to hear a poem, a good reader absorbs everything that comes with the poem. The pictures she creates in her own mind are very much a part of the reading experience, as are the illustrations that may accompany the poem. We live in a fruitful time for illustrated editions of classic poems. In the last couple of years, several beautiful volumes have been published, including Frost's *Stopping by Woods on a Snowy Evening*, Alfred Noyes's *The Highwayman*, and Henry Wadsworth Longfellow's *Hiawatha*. In addition there are on the market well-edited and illustrated poetry books for children ranging from the poetry of Carl Sandburg and e e cummings to the ballads of Robert Service.

I find these editions invaluable when teaching the poems in class. I ask the kids to compare the pictures they see in their minds when they read the poem with the one the illustrator saw.

- What part of the poem was she illustrating?
- If you were given the illustration assignment by the book company, what part would you illustrate? Why?
- Why do you think the illustrator chose this particular art medium to illustrate this poem? Why not another medium?
- What do you imagine the illustrator was thinking about as she was working on the illustration?
- What personal associations do you think she had with the poem?

By carefully examining the art accompanying a poem, children bring to light more fully their own understanding of the poem. A well-illustrated edition can help focus the poem in students' minds, pulling together what their ears hear and their eyes see. The illustration may in turn aid them in visualizing the poem, illuminating details they may have missed during reading.

Feast yourself

Eve Merriam's popular poem "How to Eat a Poem" suggests to children reading poetry that they should not be polite but "bite" into a poem. This is similar to the expression I have used with my classes when I tell them to "feast for a while." I tell them to enjoy the taste of the words in their mouths and the visions that linger in their heads *before* they try to figure out what it is they're eating. By encouraging them to feast for a while, I allow children the time to get to know a poem, which helps release their "searching-for-the-answer" gear. I help them through any difficult vocabulary and unfamiliar references and try to make thorough understanding of the poem a secondary concern.

Enjoy what you can and then together we'll see what we can discover.

DISCUSSING THE POEM

Somewhere in my faded Poetry 101 college class notes are instructions for reading poetry. They probably say something like this:

When reading a poem, notice:
- Who is the speaker of the poem?
- Where and what is the occasion of the poem?
- What is the purpose of the poem?
- What is achieved by the poem?

It all sounds great to me but a bit academic for my personality. I wonder if I'm modeling the same sort of thing when, after we have "eyeballed" a poem carefully and heard a couple of good readings of it, I ask my class wide-open questions like these:

- Okay, gang, whatcha' notice in the poem?
- What's going on in the piece?
- Who do you think might be doing the talking in the poem?
- What was the author thinking about when he wrote the poem?

The discussion afterwards gets going in all sorts of directions. Although I don't feel that we, as teachers, should completely direct the course of class interpretation of a poem, it is important that we gently edge them back if they stray too far. Take, for example, Rachel Field's "Something Told the Wild Geese":

Something told the wild geese
It was time to go.
Though the fields lay golden
Something whispered, "Snow."
Leaves were green and stirring,
Berries, luster-glossed,
But beneath warm feathers
Something cautioned, "Frost."
All the sagging orchards
Steamed with amber spice,
But each wild breast stiffened
At remembered ice.
Something told the wild geese
It was time to fly—

Summer sun was on their wings,
  Winter in their cry.

It never fails that kids' preset minds tell them that geese leave in the fall, so naturally they think the time of the poem is in the fall. I might help them to a closer reading through discourse like this:

Well, what's happening in the poem? Geese going south? Why? Something told them. Great. When? Fall? Really? Can you find a line or image to prove that? Tell you what, imagine you're a detective and you have to find the time, within a month, of the poem. What clues does the poem give you?

Soon the clues emerge: "though the fields lay golden," "leaves were green and stirring, / berries, luster-glossed" and so on. August is probably a better answer for the time of the poem.

By leading discussions like these I model how carefully a poem should be read. I create an atmosphere in which different interpretations are always accepted, but only after a close reading of the poem. Reading poetry well then becomes not an obscure skill but an attitude, an attitude that is developed through the act of reading itself. Every new poem has something to teach its readers about poetry, and the more we learn, the more proficient at learning we become.

As always Frost said it better than I do:

One reads poem A
the better to read
poem B, one reads
poem B the better
to read C, C the
better to read D
and D the better
to return and get
something more from
A.

(LATHEM AND THOMPSON 1972, ix)

EXPERIENCING THE POEM

There's a wonderful scene in the Alan Jay Lerner and Frederick Loewe musical *My Fair Lady* in which Eliza Doolittle is completely exasperated by the endless talk around her. "Words, words, words,

I'm so sick of words . . . is that all you can do?'' she expounds. ''Show me!'' she pleads.

In a way, Eliza spoke for all children. If all we do is talk about poetry and listen to poetry, poetry becomes nothing more than words, words, words. ''Show me,'' they plead. ''Let me feel the beat in my hands, sway to the rhythm with my body, feel the rhyme of the words on my tongue. Let me 'play' with the poem.'' Language play is very natural to children. Watch them on the playground. They skip rope to verbal chants and patty-cake their palms to rhyming riddles. They are actually closer to how poetry should be experienced while playing on the school ground than when sitting straight-backed in the classroom. If allowed, they will respond to poems with their whole bodies. Let them chant, gesture, clap, moan, crouch, leap, prowl, fly, snore, and sing to bring meaning to a poem. For young kids, the fun of reading a poem is in part discovering it with their bodies.

Physical movement and involvement also serve to illuminate the meaning of a poem's words and clarify its metaphors and similes. Dramatizing the imagery of a poem makes it meaningful through the children's own sensory experience. ''The Kind of Bath for Me'' (see chapter 3) is an excellent example of a poem in which kids can discover physical actions that highlight its words.

take a tub with a rub and a scrub

*look at the whirling brook
   and think about jumping in*

*chatter and shake in the
   cold black lake*

*take a dip from the
   side of a ship*

and so on.

I have the kids first find the action words in the lines (rub, scrub, whirling, jumping, chatter, shake, etc.) and then move like the action described. Helping them put all the movements together is much like choreographing the poem.

Chorusing lines and refrains *as you read or recite* a poem is also an excellent way to involve kids. It helps them focus their attention on the structure of the poem and then helps them read it themselves more meaningfully. Margaret Walker's haunting story poem ''Molly Means'' has the repeating line, ''old Molly, Molly, Molly Means,'' which I have the youngsters chorus at the end of each stanza while someone reads the poem.

Full group chorusing is equally effective in helping younger children read poetry because it allows youngsters who might be shy or timid about reading aloud to join in comfortably with the security of other voices. I refer my readers to "Seeds" in the Resources section of this book for examples of poems that might be brought to life with movement, chorusing, or dramatization. I also recommend Donna E. Norton's chapter, "Involving Children in Poetry," from her book *Through the Eyes of a Child* for even more examples and ways to stimulate children's interest in poetry (Norton 1983, 348–63).

VOICING THE POEM

One measure of your degree of understanding of a poem comes from your recitation (either from memory or from a text) of that poem. Working with a poem until it can flow from your tongue with meaning and understanding is the true test of how well you read it. A poem simply won't come comfortably off your tongue until there is a degree of personal understanding. Many secondary English teachers have told me that their real poetry classes are in oral interpretation as opposed to freshman English. Kids come to understand a poem by giving it their voices.

Being able to recite a poem requires much more than simply memorizing the sequence of words. One must internalize the intent and design of the author; become familiar with the flavor of the words, their cadence and flow; visualize the poem's imagery; and come to identify with the speaker of the poem—the very same things required in coming to understand a poem. It has been my experience that working to learn to read aloud or recite a poem accelerates my understanding of it.

When I work with youngsters in learning to recite poetry, I therefore say much the same things I would say if we were just studying the poem in class, not preparing to recite it:

- What feeling does the poem give you?
- Who is speaking in the poem?
- What images do you see in your mind? Describe them.
- How would you break the poem into "poetic breaths"?
- What experiences from your life does the poem bring to mind?

When the children have acquired a deeper understanding of the poem, I encourage them to become comfortable in performing the poem.

Enjoy its words with your audience. Let the words fascinate you as you recite.

Let your arms and body do what they feel like doing.

Punctuate the poem with your voice. Find the "illustrating expression" to use with each part of the poem.

Reciting was always a very popular part of my classes. During my morning lunch count, when I was overwhelmed with trying to keep account of who brought lunch, who was paying for hot lunch, and who had the right change, the kids would enjoy themselves playing "poetry tag." One person would start by standing up and reciting a poem and then tagging someone else for another poem. Poetry was popular not only with the kids but with their parents as well. I don't know how many times parents would comment that they couldn't believe *their* child was reciting poetry. Poetry becomes your own when you memorize it, and it is that ownership that is uniquely satisfying to students of all ages. Thomas Taelen said it well in *The Stone Circle Anthology*:

> One main kind of human wealth is what a person knows by heart. When you learn something by heart, and how to say it out loud, to voice it forth in your own manner, you grow in wealth without hurting anything, without spending or earning a penny.
> There are many excellent side effects of learning something by heart. It makes you more valuable to your friends and better company for yourself. (Taelen et al. 1984, 28)

But while I strongly urge kids to learn to recite poetry, it isn't the only way they can make a poem their own. Many of us remember the dreaded, forced memorization of our own childhoods. When my class studied Rachel Field's "Something Told the Wild Geese," for instance, some kids chose to write mini-reports on the migration of geese to make the poem their own. Others created beautiful paintings of flocks of geese. A few even used creative movement exercise to experience the poem. Poetry is like a good friend with much to offer and many different ways to be enjoyed.

WHAT POEMS SHOULD CHILDREN BE READING?

I've found one undeniable fact in education today, and that is that every child, regardless of race, creed, religion, economic background, intellectual ability, or size of ear lobes, will absolutely love the poetry of Shel Silverstein. Not only are his two books of poetry, *Where the Sidewalk Ends* and *The Light in the Attic*, perennial bestsellers, but they are universally popular with all grades. I know a teacher of slow and reading-disabled students who begins each of her reading sessions by "passing Shel." Each child in the circle reads or selects a favorite poem to be read from *Where the Sidewalk Ends*. Likewise a high school teacher I know finds Silverstein the most popular poet recited by her students in her oral interpretation class.

You would think that I would find this phenomenon exciting. I do. During my last couple of years of teaching we always did a "beatnik poetry reading," complete with sandals, dark glasses, berets, and beads, using principally—you guessed it—the poetry of Shel Silverstein. He simply is the most popular children's poet today. No child's personal library should be without Silverstein's books. No adult should be so deprived that he or she has not read at least one of Silverstein's poems.

Now that I've said that, I need to shake the earth a bit. THERE IS MORE TO POETRY THAN SHEL SILVERSTEIN. With my roof still intact, let me explain. I sense that in many schools Silverstein's two books are the entire K–6 curriculum. "Sure, we study poetry," teachers say. "We read *Where the Sidewalk Ends* every year."

"But what else?" I ask. "What about the fact that you no more need to teach children the poetry of Shel Silverstein than to give them lessons in eating McDonald's hamburgers, fries, and a shake?"

Kids love Shel, but does he challenge his readers? Does he present the types of materials that help children take that step toward becoming mature readers of poetry? Does his poetry sensitize them in their eventual response to literature? Sharpen their perceptions and enrich their lives? No, probably not all that much. But he certainly opens the door for us.

Helen Hill in an article in *The Horn Book*, "How To Tell a Sheep from a Goat—and Why It Matters," expresses my sentiments exactly.

Even an uneducated child deserves the best and no poem is good enough for children that is not good enough for adults. Nor should any poem be acceptable to adults if it does not have integrity. By integrity I mean wholeness or soundness of thought, perfection of technique, and sincerity of tone. (Hill 1979, 100–101)

To select poems simply on the basis of their popularity or their ability to induce laughter among children and thereby assure ourselves that they will sit and listen is too weak an educational stance. We must remember that the poetry we use in the classroom greatly affects the long-term impression poetry will have on children. Poetry that is too complex and abstract can leave a sour taste in children's mouths. But poetry that is too simple, too palatable, doesn't leave a taste at all after a while. If we are to help children evolve into mature readers of poetry, we must creatively challenge their imaginations and linguistic capabilities. The selection of poetry to use with children is best seen as a balance between that which they can hold and that for which they need to reach.

As much as I advocate making poetry fun and exciting, I also want it to be meaningful. I want to teach beyond the preferences of children and give them what they must strive to make their own. Our menu of poetry needs to include vegetables as well as desserts, needs to have contemporary as well as traditional poems, difficult as well as easier ones, humorous as well as serious, quaint as well as deep. Children need a broad, continuous, and imaginative exposure to the ways in which craftspeople use their language. I use Silverstein lovingly, but I turn my energies to teaching poems that children must spend time with to appreciate. I push children beyond their immediate preferences into poems that will enhance their growth as readers of poetry. Robert Frost and Carl Sandburg, Rachel Field and Stephen Vincent Benét, e e cummings and Walter De la Mare, Emily Dickinson and Langston Hughes, James Whitcomb Riley and Theodore Roethke—these are just some of the "adult" poets who can be used with children. Along with these writers there are many other fine poets who write principally for children: John Ciardi, David McCord, Jack Prelutsky, Aileen Fisher, Eloise Greenfield, Karla Kuskin, Myra Cohn Livingston, Eve Merriam, and Dennis Lee, to name a few. A more thorough listing of recommended poetry books is included in the Resources section at the end of this book.

COMING TO MEANING

The difficulty children have with some non-Silversteinian poetry is, of course, in understanding what it "means." The question of "meaning" or the interpretation of a poem is a touchy one. How

far should we, as teachers, press for a deeper meaning or understanding of an individual poem? Will too much analysis eventually
put a strangle-hold on students' appreciation of poetry?

I suspect it could—and, in many cases, has.

In my university classes and workshops, someone invariably men-
tions that staunchy, stereotypic professor who, many years before,
made him feel incredibly inadequate when his interpretation of a
poem hadn't matched the professor's verbatim.

But don't we have a responsibility to our students' growing minds
to help them grasp a more enlightened understanding of a poem?

Discovering meaning in poetry is much like looking at the "hidden face" drawings we enjoyed as kids, in which a drawing of
something such as a forest hides the outline of a human face. At
first glance, your eyes see only the trees of the forest in the scene,
but if you stare and look long enough, you can begin to discern
the features of a face. A nose here, a bit of eyebrow there. And
with those little clues, your eyes soon piece together and recognize
the entire outline of the face. Once your eyes have discovered that
face, you can never look at the drawing again without seeing it—
complete and crystal clear! Furthermore, it becomes difficult to
imagine how anyone can look at the same drawing and not see the
face, it is so apparent to you now.

A poem may appear, on first reading, to be like one of these
drawings. Nothing but trees. Through a deeper, perhaps more an-
alytical look, however, bits and pieces of a more subtle meaning,
or feelings of "there's-more-to-this-than-meets-the-eye," begin to
emerge. All of a sudden, Frost's line "miles to go before I sleep"
suggests that there may be more to his words than simply a dark,
serene passage through a wooded, wintry area. You ask, Could
"sleep" imply "death" or the end of something? If it does, what
does "darkest evening of the year" mean? And, as in looking at a
"hidden face" drawing, you use the clues you see to form a picture:

*If the eyebrows are here, then the lips need to be down here . . . if
"sleep" is death, then "miles to go" must have something to do
with a journey toward death. And so on.*

You can never read the poem again without sensing some of that
meaning. Perhaps the professor my students refer to has seen the
face in the drawing so clearly for so long that he can't imagine
anyone not seeing it. Or, perhaps, he can't fathom anyone simply
wanting only to see the trees.

What, then, should a teacher's role be in awakening the ability to see the "face" in poetry in his or her students? I suggest that we first view meaning as a process, as opposed to an end product. Interpretations and meanings are things that emerge from bits and pieces; they are not creatures born whole and correct. What we learn along the way in *coming to meaning* is certainly more valuable than our final view. Furthermore, our "final" analysis will more than likely change over time, as we absorb more knowledge and experience. Meanings in poems can come into focus as a result of a dialogue between the reader and himself, through a succession of hunches:

The reader reads the poem. He absorbs, sorts, and synthesizes the information given in the poem.	**Hmm...**
He begins to use clues, guesses, and assumptions to formulate a hypothesis about the poem.	**...I wonder if the poem is saying...**
Using the clues he tests his hypothesis.	**...No, that doesn't work so well...**
But he notices something else in the poem.	**...but wait, how about...**
He tests his revised hypothesis.	**...Yeah, now that makes better sense**

And so on until . . .

His own assumptions about the meaning match the information he sees in the poem.	**...Ah ha!**

Mr. Wordplay and Ms. Serious Poet

Another concern is, Do we need to analyze all poems? An illustration I often use with classes of students involves having two youngsters standing at opposite ends of the room. Explaining to the class that the two students represent opposite ends of a spectrum of poetry, I select one to be "Mr. Wordplay." I explain the nature of "Mr. Wordplay":

> *Mr. Wordplay loves the sounds of words—silly sounds, dilly sounds, wonderfully ridiculous sounds. It doesn't matter so much to Mr. Wordplay that his sounds don't make all that much sense. He just likes how they play on his tongue and in his ears.*

Then I recite a nonsense poem to illustrate the point. "Hickory Dickory Dock" works well. Walking across the room to the other standing student, I say, "But over here, we have Ms. Serious Poet." My hand crosses my chest with a pious gesture and I explain her nature.

> *Ms. Serious Poet is serious about her words. Every time she opens her mouth, something serious, thought-provoking, and well-said comes out. Her words talk about death and friendship, love and loss, honor and disgrace. . . . She gives us something to think about.*

I recite a more serious poem by way of demonstration. Langston Hughes's "Poem" has worked well as an example.

"But in between Mr. Wordplay and Ms. Serious Poet . . . " (I start having students form a line between the two), "we have a whole bunch of different types of poems: nursery rhymes and story poems, touching poems and sad ones, poems about nature and poems about nothing in particular—poems of every imaginable type and topic."

What I want the kids to see is that, first, there are many types of poetry and, second, that they need to be aware of the author's purpose in a particular poem. Was she like Mr. Wordplay, simply having great fun with words or was she more like Ms. Serious Poet, trying to give us something to think about? Or was she somewhere in between the two? Furthermore, when the students are writing their poetry, to which of the two are they relating most?

It is important to realize that, while beneath the lines and between the words of some poems there is a treasure house of meaning, for other poems, it is simply "what-you-hear-is-what-you-get." The type of journey I described as "coming to meaning" is unnecessary and inappropriate with Mr. Wordplay. Seeing and respecting the differences between Mr. Wordplay and Ms. Serious Poet is a valuable step in becoming a better and eventually a more discriminating reader of poetry.

A difficulty some students (and adults as well) have with poetry is that they do not grasp the spectrum of purposes in poetry between those of Mr. Wordplay and Ms. Serious Poet. They see poetry as one thing or get stuck at one end of the spectrum. They enjoy the sheer nonsense of Mr. Wordplay and are baffled, unable to begin the journey toward understanding and appreciating the poems of Ms. Serious Poet. Or they are turned off to all forms of poetry, thinking that all poetry has to be heavy with some sort of deep, hidden meaning that they, for the life of them, cannot see. Helping students to enjoy both the playfulness of words in poems that tickle their fancy and the rich, subtle meanings in other types of poems is the task of creative language arts classrooms.

Discovering Ms. Serious Poet's meaning

One thing I have always explained to my students is that some day each and every one of them will need something that Ms. Serious Poet has said. They will need a certain line or message from a poem because it will gratify them in a way that even the most comforting words of friends and family cannot. The thoughts of a certain poem will reach them as no other words can.

I remember the loss of a friend many years ago. And I remember feeling so bundled up inside with confusion and conflicting emotions that people could hardly comfort me. But it was the simple poetic thought of Langston Hughes's "Poem,"

I loved my friend
He went away from me
There's nothing more to say.
The poem ends,
Soft as it began—
I loved my friend.

that gave me solace. Simple words. A simple thought. But so meaningful to me at the time. Yes, someday we all need the words of Ms. Serious Poet.

Not all that long ago, our entire nation watched their television sets one clear winter morning to see the launching of the spaceship Challenger. It first soared, but then disintegrated and disappeared into six white streaks. The shock of the tragic loss of seven of our astronauts, one the first schoolteacher to travel in space, left us speechless. Unable to find the words to explain such a horrible happening, and still in shock, people in Kansas City read their morning newspaper a few days later to find a column by George H. Gurley, Jr., entitled "Poets Find the Words We Need." In the article, Gurley made reference to Robert Frost's "Birches." He cited the line in which Frost dreamed of climbing a birch tree toward heaven and suggested that Frost could have been speaking of man's urge to leave the earth in a spacecraft.

I'd like to get away from earth awhile
And then come back to it and begin over.

"It's natural," Gurley wrote, "to turn to poetry after the Challenger disaster because poetry attempts to deal with the incomprehensible—the relationship between the known and unknown" (Gurley 1986). Frost went on,

May no fate willfully misunderstand me
And half grant what I wish and snatch me away
Not to return. Earth's the right place for love:

The tragedy of the Challenger was, of course, that the seven astronauts were not returned to Earth. Yes, that winter morning an entire country needed what Ms. Serious Poet had written. People needed to know, in spite of all, that in the midst of a tragedy Earth is still "the right place for love."

How then can our poetry instruction help young readers begin that journey toward meaning so that when the need arises, as it must in our lives, the skills are there? How can we set the stage to help young readers evolve from the level of enjoying only the works of Mr. Wordplay to one where they are comfortable with more mature poetry? In my classrooms we kept Poetry Notebooks, which I hope helped students make those early steps toward appreciation of more mature poetry.

Poetry notebooks

An idea I developed for my classroom after hearing Lucy McCormick Calkins (*Lessons from a Child* and *The Art of Teaching Writing*) at a workshop, was to have my students keep a Poetry Notebook similar in design to her "learning logs." The notebook contained poems we were studying in class as well as personal favorites of the individual student. Along with complete poems, there were favorite images they had gathered and examples of metaphorical language. Many of the poems were broken into their poetic breaths with penciled slashes and/or were starred to show the words that carried the poetic power. The students used these notebooks when we performed poetry readings for other classes or played "poetry tag."

An obvious advantage to using the notebooks was that we could

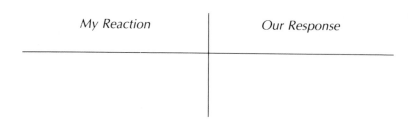

My Reaction	*Our Response*

Figure 5–1

return to a poem—make a recursive swing back to reconsider certain poems. This made it possible to rethink our initial response to a poem. With this in mind, I started using an approach similar to the one Calkins describes in her chapter on "Writing Across the Curriculum" (Calkins 1986). Choosing a poem I wanted the class to examine, I would have students glue copies of the poem in their notebooks, leaving the adjacent page blank except for two columns. One column was headed "My Reaction" and the other "Our Response" (see Figure 5–1). The students would read the poem on their own a couple of times, recording *anything* that struck them in the "My Reaction" column. I encouraged them to record *whatever* struck them—feelings or personal thoughts evoked by the poem, gut-level reactions to the poem, experimental thoughts as to what the poem might be saying, whatever!

Later when we discussed the poem as a class, the youngsters would record the garnered class responses to the poem. And, if we came back a few months later, they could record any new insights into the piece since our initial time with the poem.

This exercise accomplished a great deal. First, it respected each student's reaction to the poem. It allowed for thoughtful, personal consideration of a poem free from the getting-the-right-answer syndrome. Unlike the professor mentioned earlier, who insisted that the class embrace his understanding of a poem, I valued and respected the recorded reactions of my students. A child did not need to fear writing his own reaction, because he knew it was a working map of his journey toward meaning. Second, the class had the opportunity to nurture each other's responses through the follow-up discussion and eventual recording of "Our Response." Comments like "I never thought of that" or "Yeah, I can see that" were not uncommon.

It is my belief that no literature can be well learned in a vacuum.

Youngsters cannot read a mature poem on their own, answer comprehension questions for themselves, have their answers graded, and expect to grow in their appreciation of poetry. An aesthetic response often needs to be nurtured by a group response. We need one another. We need to test our reactions or throw our hunches and guesses out to others for their reactions. We need to merge others' insights with ours, in order to come to see the contour of the face within the forest.

Isn't it wonderful, children,
that we all can get something
different out of one poem?

It is also my belief that teachers must go only so far as students are individually comfortable in reacting to a poem. Some students are only ready to react to a poem on a literal basis and see only the forest. Fine. I, as a teacher, need to accept that, knowing that with nurturing and a continual, nonthreatening exposure to a lot of different poetry, those students will someday gain the experience to respond on a different level. As in crossing a stream, we must get our feet comfortable on the first stone before we attempt the second. Even with Ms. Serious Poet's poetry, we must get our feet steady on the literal "stone" before we step on to a more symbolic level. There must be a comfortable transition from the literal to the symbolic.

The model I perceive involves first students' individual contemplation of a poem. Then come open-ended questions about the poem in an environment in which students can relate the content of a poem to their own lives. Through this process, beginning readers can then move from a literal interpretation to a more personally directed understanding and finally (if appropriate) to a more symbolic understanding of a poem (see Figure 5–2).

I do not think that our goal is to teach students the symbolism in an individual poem. Rather, we can *allow* them to see the potential symbolic interpretation of some poetry.

Selected moments

At times, poetry seems so stuffed with meaning that getting to all of it seems impossible. Good parents never insist that their children clean the entire garage after a long winter. The task seems like an impossibility to a child. They ask, instead, if the child could help put up the tools today and next week restack the firewood. Re-

symbolic

↗

personal

↗

literal

Figure 5–2

sponding to everything in a poem all at once may seem to a child like cleaning an entire garage. I invite children to respond to selected moments in a poem, to find the line or lines to which they want to give more thought. For one class activity, I took David Wagoner's "Staying Alive," wrote the poem on a series of tagboard cards, and thumbtacked it to the classroom walls so that it wrapped around the room. Students took one line each and described what it would mean to them if they were lost in the woods. For this I used a sheet like Figure 5–3.

Using the same idea, students took one couplet from Rudyard Kipling's "If" and wrote a letter to Mr. Kipling himself, explaining

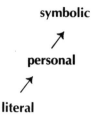

Take any line or lines from David Wagoner's "Staying Alive" and explain what it means if you were lost in the woods.

MY LINE (s) .... _____

_____

_____

WHAT IT MEANS ... _____

_____

_____

_____

_____

Figure 5–3

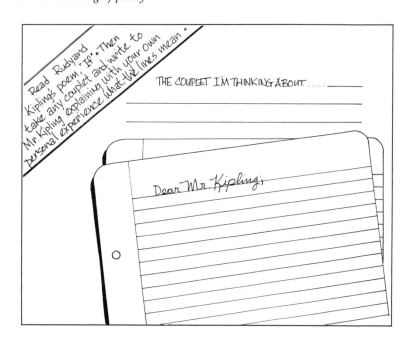

Figure 5–4

the couplet in terms of their own lives. For this I used a sheet such as Figure 5–4.

By taking one step at a time and moving comfortably from a literal to a higher level response, by taking selected moments in a poem to respond to, and by sharing responses in an atmosphere in which personal interpretation is valued above all, children *can* have meaningful experiences with Ms. Serious Poet's words. It is then that they can embark on a lifelong journey of understanding literature.

THE READING/WRITING CONNECTION

There is a final point I wish to make about the reading of poetry, and that is how it naturally stimulates and leads children into writing their own poems. If you scan the contents page in this book, you will see that "The Reading of Poetry" and "The Writing of Poetry" are presented as separate parts. I have written about each concept individually only so that I could direct my attention to one area at a time—not so that they would necessarily be taught as separate activities or subjects. It has been my experience that the prime time for youngsters to write poetry is directly following their reading of poetry.

Reading poetry and writing poetry facilitate each other. Reading a poem well, discovering some of its craft, and sensing the author's design, spills over comfortably into the writing of a similar poem. And by the act of writing, by applying her own poetic skills, the writer comes to understand the original poem better. Whereas examining a poem provides the reader with poetic ideas, word patterns, and fuel for her poetic imagination, attempting to write a similar poem sheds light back on the original piece. The interaction of the reading and writing often helps students achieve a level of understanding that might otherwise have been impossible.

It might interest you to know that most accomplished writers first modeled their writing after someone else. The early novels of Jack Kerouac, for example, were modeled very closely on the work of Thomas Wolfe. Often this period of a writer's development is known as the "apprentice stage." By modeling their writing of poems after a poem they have read, children "role play" as writers.

The poet's invisible hand

Having children model their poetry after something they have read relieves them of the anxiety of having to conceptualize the entire idea. They can first be stimulated by a poem. Then, using the structure of the poem and plugging in their own words and ideas, they can become practicing "poets." I discuss this process with youngsters as "the poet's invisible hand guiding our hands into authorship."

Notice how easily the poet's invisible hand guided this kindergartner into authorship:

Higglety, Pigglety Pop!
The dog has eaten the mop;
*   The pig's in a hurry,*
*   The cat's in a flurry,*
Higglety, pigglety, pop!

                    (SAMUEL GOODRICH, "Higglety, Pigglety Pop")

Higglety, Pigglety <u>Pan</u>
The dog has eaten the <u>man</u>
*   The* <u>goat's</u> *in a hurry,*

The bird's *in a flurry,*
Higglety, Pigglety Pan*!*

Another youngster became an author with this jump-rope rhyme:

Teddy Bear
Teddy Bear turn around
Teddy Bear, Teddy Bear touch the ground
Teddy Bear, Teddy Bear tie your shoe,
Teddy Bear, Teddy Bear I love you.

Teddy Bear
Teddy Bear sing a song
Teddy Bear, Teddy Bear run along
Teddy Bear, Teddy Bear walk this way
Teddy Bear, Teddy Bear climb all day.

The very successful work Kenneth Koch has done with children
writing poetry demonstrates how effective modeling can be. In his
classic *Wishes, Lies and Dreams,* he uses a model of "poetry ideas"
to help his students write poetry. Models such as "Wishes" ("I wish
I was an apple / I wish I was a steel apple"), and "comparisons"
("A flag is like a balloon flying the sky"), and "I used to / but now"
("I used to want to be a baseball player with my brother / But now
I want to be a dancer") were used as writing springboards to open
up their writing and help them discover new ways of saying things
(Koch 1970).

Using the idea of a "class collaboration" also developed by Koch,
I guided my second graders in writing our own type of comparison
poem after a day hike in the mountains:

IN THE WOODS

In the woods I smell good
clean air instead of dirty
polluted air.

In the woods I can hear water
rushing and not desks
moving.

In the woods I like hearing
a good story and not
the teacher teaching spelling.

*In the woods I smell nice
    fresh air and not
    stinky old school air.*

*In the woods I feel bumpy
    rocks and not hard
    pencils.*

*In the woods I see prickly
    pine trees and not hard,
    hard work.*

*In the woods I feel fresh
    and not tired like at
    school.*

*In the woods I hear water
    rushing with the cool breeze
    and not feet trooping
    up and down the stairs.*

*In the woods I see singing
    woodpeckers and not white
    chalk.*

*In the woods I see pretty
    blackbirds and not
    green blackboards.*

We used the same collaboration idea later that year with "Christ-mas Poem." Here we attempted some rhyming couplets:

CHRISTMAS POEM

*I dream at Christmas time . . .
    of packages bright and gay
    and songs the reindeer say,*

*of presents all around me
    and I'll open them with a secret key.*

*I dream at Christmas time . . .
    that little brothers are sweet
    and maybe they can be a treat,*

*of hearing a reindeer on my house
    but it was just a great big mouse.*

I dream at Christmas time . . .
  that I see toys everywhere with my name
  and a picture of my aunt with a frame,

  that I found 24 dollars under a tree
  that Santa Claus gave me.

I dream at Christmas time . . .
  of bees that will pop out of a box
  and a giant stuffed ox,

  that I got a dog
  which looked exactly like a frog.

I dream at Christmas time . . .
  that we are so happy
  we have to hurry to make it snappy,

  there's a Christmas tree by me
  but only three toys do I see.

I dream at Christmas time . . .
  that my family is a special treat
  so we have to be extra sweet,

  of making a song called "Christmas Time"
  and it will be all mine.

I dream at Christmas time . . .
  about stockings hung about
  and packages of great amounts,

  of Christmas being white with snow
  and it will blow.

In his second book, *Rose, Where Did You Get That Red?—Teaching Great Poetry to Children*, Koch takes his method even further by having youngsters model their poetry on the work of adult poets from William Blake to Federico García Lorca. The ideas posed in the adult poems present the framework within which the kids can then paint with their own language and experiences. In the same vein, Kate Farrell teamed up with Koch to write *Sleeping on the Wing*, producing another book in which adult poems from Whitman to Williams, from Dickinson to Pound, are used to stimulate poetic responses from students. If you haven't already read these books, I recommend them to you.

Picture books are also easy models for beginning writers to use in testing their wings as poets. Charlotte Zolotow's *Someday* and *If*

It Weren't for You made their way into my third graders' writing class. The following example was modeled after *Someday*:

SOMEDAY when I go to school my
  teacher would say, "You're
  the only one that can do it right."

SOMEDAY when I run a race, it is
  going to be called,
  "The Jogging Race."

SOMEDAY when I have a lot of
  money, I would buy a bed and
  a dresser with a chair.

SOMEDAY my parents are going
  to give rights for anything
  I want.

SOMEDAY at home, my house is
  going to be painted white;
  it's going to get new grass.

SOMEDAY on my birthday my mom
  is going to take me on a trip
  to Hawaii and let me go
  to Chicago and all over the world.

SOMEDAY I would like to be
  a fairy that flies across the sky
  and gives people wishes.

SOMEDAY when I go to school I will
  have ice cream at lunchtime.

SOMEDAY when I have a lot of money
  I will spend it on candy.

SOMEDAY my parents would say,
  "You can take all the money."

SOMEDAY at home I would have an extra
  room for me that has a lock on it.

SOMEDAY on Christmas, I will get more
  presents.

The next example was modeled after Charlotte Zolotow's *If It Weren't For You*:

If it weren't for you,
    I wouldn't have to eat a good supper
    and eat candy instead
    and never get in trouble.

If it weren't for you,
    I'd never have to cut my hair
    and get all the "goodies" from
    the Christmas tree
    instead of just my share.

If it weren't for you,
    I could ride my bike as far as
    I wanted and not have to
    go to bed at 8:00.

If it weren't for you
    I could stay up and watch
    "Shock Theatre"
    and go to the zoo without you.

If it weren't for you,
    I could swim everyday, see T.V.
    and "Star Wars" whenever I wanted,
    eating popcorn instead of
        beef jerky.

If it weren't for you,
    I could jump in the mud with a thud
    and buy every toy I wanted to,
    but never have to go to the
        dentist.

If it weren't for you,
    I'd never have to go to the
    doctor for shots
    and we would never have
        squash.

BUT if it weren't for you,
    I wouldn't be here!!

There are varying levels at which children can use poetic models in their writing. As with "Higglety, Pigglety Pop" and "Teddy Bear, Teddy Bear," the easiest way for younger students to get started is by substituting their own rhyming words in a poem. A group of first graders enjoyed discovering the "golden thread" woven into the rhyme scheme of Dennis Lee's "Alligator Pie" (first mentioned in chapter 3), reproduced here in its entirety:

Alligator pie, alligator pie,
If I don't get some I think I'm gonna die.
Give away the green grass, give away the sky,
But don't give away my alligator pie.

Alligator stew, alligator stew,
If I don't get some I don't know what I'll do.
Give away my furry hat, give away my shoe,
But don't give away my alligator stew.

Alligator soup, alligator soup,
If I don't get some I think I'm gonna droop.
Give away my hockey stick, give away my hoop,
But don't give away my alligator soup.

Then, by weaving their own tapestry of rhythm and rhyme, they created their own poems:

Alligator coke, alligator coke,
If I don't get some I think I'm gonna croak.
Give away my socks, give away my cloak,
But don't give away my alligator coke.

Alligator cake, alligator cake,
If I don't get some I think I'm gonna shake.
Give away my lizard, give away my snake,
But don't give away my alligator cake.

Alligator juice, alligator juice,
If I don't get some I'll turn my dog loose.
Give away my monkey, give away my moose,
But don't give away my alligator juice.

Easily the most popular model book is Mary O'Neill's *Hailstones and Halibut Bones* (mentioned in chapter 3). Here is a fourth grader's rendering of the color red:

WHAT IS RED?

Red is a plump juicy dark red apple.
Red is the beauty of a rainbow bursting with colors.
Red is a river running soft on a beautiful waterfall.
Red is leaves falling off a beautiful big tree.

And, here, a sixth grader's idea of white:

WHITE IS . . .

A dove who is a figure of grace
    A glove all fancy and laced
Edelweiss sprinkled with dew
    An apple blossom given to you
An angel so very innocent
    A unicorn so powerful and magnificent
The wind that has such power
    The sweet scent of a flower.

Some modeling, however, requires a deeper, more complete understanding of the poem modeled. For example, on one of our return
loops to David Wagoner's "Staying Alive" (also mentioned in chapter 3), my fifth graders' follow-up discussion deviated from looking
at the poem as simply being about survival in the woods. We took
a step from the literal stepping stone to a different view of the poem.
We discussed how many of the points made in the poem could be
interpreted to mean more than survival in the woods: surviving in
a large family, surviving in junior high, surviving in a ghetto. Following the design of the poem and locking in on the pulse of its
rhythm, we mimicked the poem using the theme of staying alive in
the classroom. (To truly appreciate this, you may need to reread
Wagoner's original piece on page 49.)

Staying alive in a classroom is a matter
Of calming down at first and deciding whether
To wait for recess, trusting the bell will ring,
Or simply to start talking and talking in one direction
Till you finish—or the principal happens to stop you.
By far the safer choice
Is to settle down where you are, and try to make
A go of the books you read, staying near a clock,
Away from bad report cards.
It may be best to learn what you have to learn with

A teacher. Not killing them but watching them and
Their yardsticks go
In and out of shelter
At will. Following their teaching, build knowledge for a
lifetime.
Facing across the wind in your pile of homework,
You may feel worse.
But nothing, not even you, can do anything about it.

Take no drugs,
Spit out all bitterness. Shooting at Math books
Means hiking further for more.
If you hurt yourself,
Studying, working, and reading no one will comfort you or
Do your homework for you.

Ubi sunts

Often the idea suggested by a poem can be used to stimulate writing. I remember once preparing a reading lesson plan with David McCord's "Where" (again, see chapter 3) and being struck by the fact that his poem reminded me of the medieval "ubi sunts" from my undergraduate days. "Ubi sunt" is Latin for "where are they" and represents an old type of poetry that lamented something in the past.

Where are the days gone past?
Where are my old friends?

The earliest example of the ubi sunt is an Old English poem "The Wanderer," in which an aging soldier laments his old comrades in arms with words something like these:

Where are those who died alongside me in battle . . .
Where are the great mead halls . . .
Where are the great fields of battle . . .

A more recent example of the use of the ubi sunt appears in Edgar Lee Master's "Spoon River Anthology." Here the poet laments those who have lived and died in a town called Spoon River:

Where are Elmer, Herman, Bert, Tom and Charley,
The weak of will, the strong of arm, the clown, the boozer, the
fighter?
All, all are sleeping on the hill.

The hill obviously is the graveyard and as the poem goes on, the
characters rise from their graves to tell their own stories.

Using the idea of the ubi sunt, we played with David McCord's
"Where" as a model for our own ubi sunts. The kids thought that
writing poetry with a name like that was really "something." Here
are some of their thoughts:

Where is my chair for sitting?
Where is my table for resting?
Where is my book for opening?
Where are the words for reading?
Where are my glasses for seeing?
Where are . . . ?
　　　Well, anyway, I don't have a book.

Where is the ski slope I wish for?
Why doesn't it snow some more?
Where is my money for the lift?
Maybe I'll get it for a gift.
Where is my scarf and mittens?
The ones that are furry like kittens.
Where is my coat and hat?
I couldn't go without them.
Where is my long underwear?
The one with the big tear?
Where is . . . ?
　　　Well, anyway, it's summer.

It was fun explaining to the kids this time that the poet's invisible,
guiding hand came all the way from the annals of English literary
history.

While pattern books and poem models provide an accessible way
of connecting the reading and writing acts of poetry, I fear that
sometimes their products become an end in themselves. Children
may become convinced that they have truly written original poetry.
They may believe, in finding a pattern and duplicating it with a few
of their own changes, that that's all there is to writing poems. Furthermore, teachers may believe that, with a few creative outbursts

based on a pattern book or two, their yearly requirement for poetry writing instruction is fulfilled. I have visited countless middle schools and junior high schools in which the entire poetry-writing curriculum is solely centered around Koch's "Wishes," "Comparisons," and "Dreams" poems.

True poetry-writing instruction allows children to tap their own imaginations to discover a startling new image, a different way of looking at the ordinary, or an intriguing arrangement of words. Pattern books, model poems, and formulated poetry writing gimmicks are certainly allies to beginning writers, but they can never substitute for students' own original poetic endeavors. Our students need to develop their own "poetic ears," their own style, and their own voices, and this can only be accomplished when they attempt their own poems. We learn to write by writing! Pattern books and models are best viewed as part of an "apprentice stage" in which students take those first tentative steps into writing. I hope the next chapter can make the successive steps less of a struggle.

Before leaving this section, I'd like to share a poem entitled "811" that I wrote and kept in my students' poetry corner with all our poetry books. For those of you who have forgotten your Dewey decimal system, 811 is the call number for books of poetry in your library.

811

Reading a poem well
is much more than simply reading it.

We experience it—
our eyes and ears and tongue
come together

to see, hear and voice
what the poet has created.

We may be moved
or tricked
or amused
or simply drawn into wonderment
of its sounds.

But if we open up completely
to what the poem has to offer—
to feel it with our whole bodies—

and release our imaginative-selves
to its spell
   (if only for a moment)
Then we have read the poem well
and are free to take all that it has to give.

Now, on to the writing of poetry.

THE WRITING OF POETRY

. . . apprenticeship in wordsmithing

WRITERS-OF-WORDS BY TRADE

Once in a small village there were two men, each a writer-of-words by trade. And in most ways these two writers-of-words appeared to be identical. Both had studied and practiced their craft well; both had many fine, sharp-pointed feather quills and stained bottles of black ink; and both sat in their studies long hours carefully composing and writing out their words on sheets of parchment, which the villagers then could read. So, from all appearances, it was as if these writers-of-words did the very same thing: write words. But the people of the village knew that each was different from the other—born under the same night sky but facing different stars.

The first writer-of-words was a chronicler of facts. If one of the village couples was blessed with a child, his words clearly announced the necessary facts (boy, brown hair, born after midnight on Wednesday). If there was a dispute among two of the village farmers, his words presented each side of the disagreement (whose cow, which fence), with carefully obtained and logically presented information.

Before writing, the first writer would breathe deeply and lay out all of his information before him. He would decide which fact was the most important and therefore what the villagers needed to know first. He chose the simplest, most direct words he could find to present this information. The first writer-of-words was skilled in eliminating any words that might confuse or possibly mislead the village readers. He prided himself on always using words so clear and to the point that the villagers never once needed to ask him the meaning of something he had written. They knew exactly what was happening in their village, thanks to the words of the first writer. There was no question that the first writer-of-words was indeed a good, skilled writer-of-words!—an asset to the village.

The second writer-of-words was somehow different. To him words and word expressions were like bends in an unexplored path waiting to be discovered by curious children. While the first writer always knew exactly where he was going by having all the information clearly laid out in front of him before he started composing and arranging his words, the second often just started writing to see what he could discover around the next bend. Sometimes he would begin his writing with only a faint idea or impression or catchy combination of words in his head. At times the second writer-of-words appeared more concerned with how his words sounded inside his head than with the literal truth of his information. If "crimson" sounded better beside "crown" than "brown," then "crimson crown" it was, regardless of whether the crown was crimson or brown, or blue-silver. He had no problem changing a fact in his writing to make a more interesting image, a more tuneful arrangement of his words.

Some of the villagers whose eyes had peered into the study window of the second writer-of-words had seen him rearranging a group of words many, many times, each time saying the words out loud, frowning and shaking his head, and trying another arrangement. They had even seen him try six different words that meant the same thing until he found just the word he wanted. "Why doesn't he just use the one with the right meaning?" they asked. One villager swears that the second writer-of-words made up a brand new word because he couldn't find one he liked.

Some of the villagers even suggested that the second writer-of-words had fairy dust in his eyes for he saw the world in such strange and wonderful ways. To him a leaf falling from one of the village trees was a tear or the loss of a dream; a falling star, a vision.

For the second writer-of-words was more than just a writer. He was a craftsman of words—a wordsmith. He did with words what the village wood carver did with a knotted piece of driftwood when he began carving and shaving off bits and pieces of wood with his chisel until a beautiful figure began to emerge. And the wordsmith was like the village musician as he puttered and played with musical notes until the beginnings of a melody appeared. So by his carving and puttering and playing the wordsmith created wonderful works that the villagers could enjoy. He tried never to have his words *tell* about a feeling he was having; he wanted whoever read his words to *feel what he felt*—to touch what he had touched, to see what he had seen. Unlike the first writer-of-words, who wanted his words to give current information, the wordsmith wanted his words to become timeless and to stick in the heads and hearts of the villagers. The wordsmith dreamed that his words would live beyond him.

So it was a happy village with both a writer and a wordsmith. Sometimes the first writer-of-word's words were needed and sometimes the wordsmith's words were needed. At town meetings and in the village court the first writer-of-word's words were indispensable. But at weddings or other such occasions the wordsmith's special words were needed to express the appropriate sentiment. Also at those rare moments of despair or sorrow the wordsmith's words were called up to give solace. And so it was that the first writer's words served their purpose well, and the words of the wordsmith served their special purpose.

WORDSMITHING

Poetry is written by writers, but not all writers write poetry. All share the same tools and appear outwardly to be doing the same thing, but their use of the language can be different—as it was for the two writers in my story. The first writer was concerned primarily with presenting information, while the wordsmith—the poet—focused on the resources of language: the attention brought to a phrase by the repetition of similar sounds; the element of surprise that unusual combinations of words can achieve; the visual effect created by the placement of words on the page; the subtle but intriguing impact that line breaks can have; the power of a few well-chosen words; and the insights made possible by the use of metaphors. These are the things about language that fascinate poets.

This is not to suggest that poets use imagery, figurative language, rhythm, and rhyme every time they take pencil in hand, nor is it to imply that they are oblivious to offering information to the reader. I suggest only that, in their writing, poets are acutely sensitive to the resources of language and particularly conscious of how to use those resources to suit their purposes.

Perhaps I can best illustrate this with a simple example from my own writing. A few years ago I was writing a fairy tale. It began:

> Once upon a time long ago, when
> there was still magic in the kingdoms
> and forests, there lived a man and
> a woman. They had twin sons.

I was focusing my attention on making sure the reader got the necessary information: that the story was taking place long ago, in a fairy-tale setting; that magic would be a part of the story; that the characters were a man and a woman; and that they had sons who were twins. I had accomplished what I wanted. I had given the information.

Later, as my writing mind began to work more like the word-smith's, focusing on language and its possibilities, I drafted a new beginning:

> *In a time*
> *quite distant*
> *from ours now . . .*
>
> *when the kingdoms and forests*
> *were still*
> *held captive*
> *to the whims of mystery*
> *and enchantment,*

there lived a man
and a woman
who had twin sons.

So, what was the difference between the two drafts? Both had given the reader the same information. Why was I more satisfied with the second version? Because in it I had played a bit more with the words, and as a result I had used the language in a more dramatic way. I had attempted not only to express my meaning, but also to arouse the imagination of my readers. Notice how "quite distant / from ours now" and "were still / held captive" create an eerie mood for the story's beginning. I liked the sound of "whims of mystery," created by the *ms* sound of "whims" playing off the *mys* sound of "mystery," and felt that it gave a rolling, rhythmic feeling to that line. By adopting some of the writing behavior of the wordsmith, I had attempted to explore what is possible with language.

I doubt seriously whether a poet consciously sits down at her desk and says to herself, "This is Wednesday, and I'm a poet, so today I'll write using metaphors and similes." The poet uses a metaphor or simile when and only when it suits the purposes of her writing. However, "Today-is-Wednesday-and-we-are-going-to-write-a-poem-using-one-metaphor-or-simile" is the approach taken by some well-intentioned teachers.

These teachers pass out sheets with fill-in-the-blank statements:

A cloud is like _____.

The kids then fill in with words like "cotton" or "popcorn" and add a qualifier and have a poem, quick and easy.

The sky
is like
popcorn
all popped up.

I do not intend to be overly critical of such a teacher or of the child's effort. In fact, I sort of like the poem and I am sure that I used a similar procedure in many of my own lessons. What I'm suggesting is that this approach, if used exclusively, is too mechanical and product-oriented. It separates the child writer from a fuller participation in the writing process. It guarantees the teacher some clever poems to put on the bulletin board, while denying children the chance to experience the excitement and surprise of capturing their thoughts with their own words. Furthermore, they get little practice in actual wordsmithing.

"Recipe" types of writing instruction, such as the poem-with-one-metaphor, appeal to many teachers because, in their experience, children on their own show little skill in producing or sustaining poetic techniques in their writing. And they are right: children are highly erratic and undisciplined in their attempts to write poetry. Consequently, their efforts appear to produce little of value, while use of the "recipe" produces at least what one can call a poem. But, in order for children to grow as writers and along the way to acquire the confidence and maturity to share their unique perspective of the world, they must first come to understand and gain practice in how writers go about their craft. In short, they must be allowed to discover what it is they want to say and how they want to go about saying it . . . even if their end products along the way are uneven. A premium might well be placed on how much of the poet's craft the children attempted each time—*not* on whether they created a "poem."

As students gain more control and proficiency as writers, specific poetry-writing instruction should be centered on having students internalize the writing style of poets (adopting the behavior of my second writer-of-words) and become apprentices in the craft of wordsmithing. If I had my way, we would call our poetry-writing workshops "Beginning Wordsmithing," "Wordsmithing I," "Wordsmithing II," and "Advanced Wordsmithing." The emphasis would then be on experimenting with and practicing the poet's craft, understanding the poet's concerns and focuses, and developing an appreciation for the resources available within our rich language . . . not simply on producing a poem.

I will always remember the fifth grader who barged into my classroom the first day of school. Knowing my reputation for emphasizing poetry, he confronted me. "Hey, Mr. Denman, are we gonna have to write a poem this year?"

In one of those rare moments, I had the perfect response. I smiled. "Heavens, no, my friend, we'll be too busy learning wordsmithing to write any poetry."

It may be helpful for the reader to note that the remainder of this chapter will progress from discussions and activities geared toward primary-age youngsters to those appropriate for intermediate-through middle- and junior high school students (broadly and lovingly referred to as "older kids"). As with any subject area, teaching styles and instructional strategies change as the maturity and language experiences of the students evolve. However, the underlying approach I used in all my classes, whether they were made up of shy and wide-eyed kindergartners or rough-and-ready seventh graders, was to teach the writing of poetry as a craft—a craft I referred to as "wordsmithing." I tried to make all my students aware, regardless of their ages, of how a poet thinks and works, and in so doing, to encourage them to try on for size those writing habits when they attempted their own poetry.

And so, as I'm sure you will all remember from your physical education classes, when you had to line up in the gym . . . "We'll begin with the shortest kids."

PRIMARY KIDS—CONNECTING POEMS AND PRINT

If children are to mature into writers and wordsmiths, they must be saturated early in life with examples of printed language worthy of their attention and satisfying to their imaginations. They must sense, even before they can actually read, the power and beauty of that language. They need to make a connection between spoken words and printed words. They need to see that the marks on a book's page, on the sides of cereal boxes, or on billboards outside the car windows all convey meaning. They need to realize that the rounds they sing, the nonsense rhymes they recite, and the playground chants they scream have a correspondence to printed letters on a page. To accomplish this, our classrooms need to become literary communities where children become increasingly familiar and delighted with many forms of written language.

Saturate and celebrate

A saying I am fond of using in my poetry workshops and classes with older kids is:

Becoming a poet
is coming to take notice
of how poets—
yourself included—
use words.

Developing a poet's habit of "coming to notice" begins very early in school.

Good morning, children,
nice to see you.
For your eyes' and ears'
pleasure today,
we'll start with a poem.

In my primary classrooms, I took long sheets of butcher paper, wrote out the words to a poem with a colorful Magic Marker, and attached the sheet to a hanger (see Figure 6–1). I then stored a collection of poems by hanging them on a rack and allowed the kids to choose one with which to begin each day. They could hang the poem in front of the class for everyone to see and enjoy. On a snowy day we hung Dorothy Aldis's poem entitled, appropriately, "On a Snowy Day."

Each child had a writing book stapled together with sheets of both wide-lined and unlined paper and a colorful cover titled, in bold print, *My Writing Book,* into which they would copy the words of the poem. Together we would celebrate the poem—singing and clapping to its unique sounds. Together we would cultivate a beginning appreciation of the craft behind the words. And together we would begin building pathways into printed poetry.

Who can show me his
favorite word in the whole poem?
The best sounding word?
The words that give us the best picture?
The action words?
The rhyming words?
We'll put stars over our favorite words.
Who can show me where we breathe
when we read the poem?
We'll draw a big slash here to remind us
to take a breath.

Who has a different picture in his head
of a "snowy day"?
Let's find the words for that picture.
We'll write them here
so we can look at them during the day.
Isn't it interesting how we can create
pictures in our heads with the words we use?
Let's copy the words of the poem in our writing books
in case we want to think or write more about it later.

On a Snowy Day

Fence posts wear marshmallow hats
On a winter's day,
Bushes in their nightgowns
Are kneeling down to pray,
And trees spread out their snowy skirts
Before they dance away.

Figure 6–1

My bulletin boards would be a gathering of what I labeled "word wonderments" to catch the children's roving eyes. "Word wonderments" were our favorite words from poems, songs, rhymes, and stories, which we colored and designed with bright Magic Markers. "Spring is showery, flowery, bowery" from the poem "Our Seasons" (author unknown) was an example of what might appear on our "word wonderment" bulletin board. As the children came to know these phrases and to make connections between the verses and their special words, they would be on the lookout for other examples of "word wonderments" in their own listening, reading, and writing. Their first poems were "whisper thoughts" whispered into my ear, which I scripted for them and added to the bulletin board. They began to develop preferences—what they liked and what intrigued them about words. We joyfully and intentionally celebrated each other's discoveries in language.

> *Oh, children, look at*
> *this fine word wonderment*
> *that Sarah discovered.*
> *Let's put it on the board*
> *and in our writing books.*

Along our pathway into poetry, we would take time to examine how printed language can be used creatively. We noticed how John Archambault dropped the letters of the "drip" in his poem "Ice Cream."

> *Children, can you see*
> *why he wrote his poem that way?*

ICE CREAM

> *There's nothing like it*
> *on a hot summer day,*
> *but you gotta lick quick*
> *before it melts away!*

> *Lickety, lick,*
> *Lick lick real quick—*
> *Before it goes*
> *drip drip*
> *drip*
> *d*
>   *r*
>   *i*
>   *p*
>   *!*

The children then experimented with this idea in their own writing.

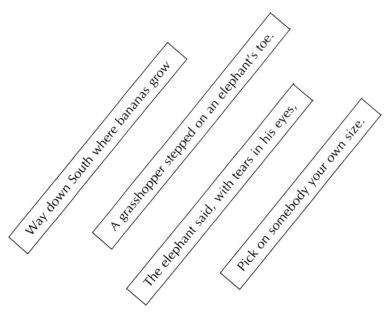

Figure 6–2

Or we would cut up the different lines of a poem and mix them up and see if by using our "sense of sound" we could put the poem back together again. "Way Down South," by an anonymous author, is a good poem for this type of activity. (See Figure 6–2).

We became familiar with rhyming words through rhyming riddles:

- Something you do when you play tag—rhymes with fun.
- Something you wear—it rhymes with bat.
- Something that stings—rhymes with tree.
- Something to eat—rhymes with dandy.
- A machine that you ride in—rhymes with fuss.

And then we made up our own rhymes with animals:

A snake named Sloan
Ate an ice cream cone.

A moose named Harry
Has a girlfriend named Mary.

A rabbit named Jenny
  Would like a new penny.

A giraffe named Jan
  Ran over a pan.

A raccoon named Peg
  Walked on her leg.

A seal named Dan
  Got in a van.

An owl named Mo
  Makes his eyes glow.

Together we enjoyed the popcorn-popping sounds created by this poem:

POPCORN

Pop	*pippty pop*
ping	*pippty pop*
pop ping	*pippity pippity*
pop pip	*popp popp*
pip pop	*mounds of*
popping	*white kernels*
white grains	*mounds of*
growing	*fluffy white*
popping	*crackling chewy popped corn.*

(Author unknown)

Isn't it interesting, children, that words
can make the same sounds as popping popcorn?
Let's listen for other words that describe sounds.
We'll put a list of them in our writing books.
We'll listen to the real sounds of popping popcorn
while we write.

In a circle on the floor, we acted out the specific details described in Mary Britton Miller's poem "Cat," distinguishing between words that show parts of the cat and words that describe actions. One of the students brought his cat from home to our reading center, and we watched its actions, matching phrases with what we saw.

CAT

The black cat yawns,
Opens her jaws,
Stretches her legs,
And shows her claws.

Then she gets up
And stands on four
Long stiff legs
And yawns some more.

She shows her sharp teeth,
She stretches her lip,
Her slice of a tongue
Turns up at the tip.

Lifting herself
On her delicate toes,
She arches her back
As high as it goes.

She lets herself down
With particular care,
And pads away
With her tail in the air.

Now, I wonder if we can find words that describe
how we look on the playground.
We'll put them in our writing books.

Through a series of similar encounters with words, children discover that words are worth their attention and effort. They begin to acquire a taste for printed language. They savor those words and expressions that appeal to their sensibilities by singing and repeating them over and over to themselves on the playground and in their backyards. They discover a connection between the pleasure in the oral manipulation of sounds and in doodling with pencil and paper. In doing so they attempt to represent their word musings on paper by drawing pictures and symbols for words. They invent wild spellings and devise colorful ways of making their letters and punctuation marks correspond to what they feel and want them to say. More than likely, they will insist that you listen to their "poems." Their writing books become cluttered scrapbooks of drawings and oddly formed letters. "My poems," they proudly say. They have indeed started their apprenticeship in wordsmithing. They are on their own pathways into poetry.

It is believed that children can acquire up to thirty new words a day from the environment around them. If we as classroom teachers are aware of this remarkable phenomenon, we can nurture these expanding vocabularies. Daily exposure to bits and pieces of poetry and rhyme, story and verse, can lead to the emergence of a true literary community within our classrooms. In such a rich environment, children joyously make the first connections between spoken and printed language. In so doing, they embark on a lifelong journey as speakers, readers, and writers who are sensitive to words.

First steps

The connection between the stories, poems, and songs children hear and the printed words they see creates in them the desire to use this written language to express their own thoughts. Their desire is strong, but there are many obstacles. Even using a pencil may require more physical control than they have. When it becomes apparent that independent writing requires skill in visual discrimination, sequencing, and recall, the task may seem nearly overwhelming. Words, which seemed to be a wide open door into the world of written language, may suddenly become barricades to the enjoyment of writing.

In my primary classroom, I tried to circumvent these difficulties inherent in early writing development. I gave attention instead to broader, but less frustrating, concerns: writing ideas, personal satisfaction, and word play—what to write about, how to express one's thoughts comfortably, and how to manipulate words and phrases freely. These became the focus of my writing lessons. Students used invented spellings and word pictures as freely as they did crayons, Magic Markers, and big, heavy red pencils. Individual students who might otherwise have been struggling alone with the mechanics of writing involved themselves in class writing and spoken dictation to their scripters, or "writing buddies."

Each month my bulletin board was a collection of words and pictures: "Writing Ideas for the Month." Michael got a new puppy one month, so *puppy* and *Ralphy* and *pets* went up on the board with bright Magic Markers. Later in the month, we read a story about dinosaurs, so *dinosaur* and pictures of prehistoric times found their way to the board. If there were tacos for lunch in the cafeteria, *taco*, other related food phrases, and delectable-looking pictures of associated foods were placed on the board.

Our first poems were class poems, written as a group. Each child contributed a line, which was written down exactly as the child spoke it. On one snowy day, looking out the window, we wrote:

IF I WERE A SNOWFLAKE

> *If I were a snowflake,*
>   *I'd be kind of small and*
>   *I'd come down slowly.*
>   *I'd flutter—I'd be lighter than a feather.*
>   *I'd feel like I was flying—*
>   *I'd fall and get a headache.*
>   *I'd freeze!*
>   *I'd turn into a piece of ice*
>   *Then I'd freeze into an icicle.*
>   *When I hit the ground,*
>   *I'd break or*
>   *I'd fall down and melt.*
>   *I'd probably get stuck in a tree,*
>   *I might land on top of a dog or*
>   *Maybe fall into a cat's mouth.*
>   *If I landed on a piece of grass it would*
>   *prick me.*
>   *Santa's reindeer would trample me.*
>   *I'd want to be part of a snowman.*
>   *(Probably someone would pick me up and throw me!)*

Later, with another class collaboration, I showed the students how we could work at wordsmithing by changing or adding a word or two to create an interesting "sounding" line. "*Being in a boat*" was shaped into "*Fun in a boat, all afloat.*" Here are a couple of lines from "Happiness," a poem the class and I created:

> *Fun in a boat, all afloat,*
> *Staying with my dad, he's bad,*
> *A cat and a house, a puppy and*
>   *a mouse,*
> *Riding on a horse, of course,*
> *Food, food, food, Oh-oo!*

To free very young children from the tiring effort of writing out a whole thought, I solicited the help of parents and older students to take dictation. Lying on their backs in the park, with their "writing buddies" close at hand, these first graders dictated:

I see
in the clouds
a volcano
bursting into the air.

I see
in the clouds
a giant wave
covering a mountain
with a white and blue quilt.

Back in the classroom, the students copied their poems onto sheets of art paper covered with tempera clouds, and we shared them orally and visually with other classes.

In our early experimentation with poetic form, we used a variety of forms that allowed the children to play with words within a linguistic structure. Here is an example of an "inverted poem" I wrote, in which I added one word (or so) with each successive line. We preferred to call these "add-a-word" poems.

PIG

A pig
A fat pig
A muddy, fat pig
A muddy, fat, pink pig
A muddy, fat, wrinkled, pink pig
A muddy, fat, wrinkled, pinkled, pink pig
A muddy, fuddy, fat, wrinkled, pinkled, pink pig
A muddy, ruddy, fuddy, fat, wrinkled, pinkled, pink pig
A muddy, ruddy, fuddy, fat, wrinkled, pinkled pick of a pink pig
A pig

After chorusing the poem and clapping out its rhythm, I discussed wordsmithing with the youngsters:

Children, look at this line:
"A muddy, fat, wrinkled, pinkled, pink pig."
Let's cut out all the individual words
and put them on cards with markers, so
we can spread them out on the floor and

arrange and rearrange them
the way we like.

Isn't it interesting that
by changing the arrangement,
we can change the music
of the line?
Which way sounds best to you?
Why do you think I used the word
"pinkled"? Do you like its sound?
Can you think of some more "made up" words
we could use?

Together and individually, we experimented with other "add-a-word" poems:

> TRUCK
> A truck
> A dirty truck
> A dirty, dented truck
> A dirty, dented, green truck
> An old, dirty, dented, green truck
> An old, dirty, dented, green truck . . .
> that I have to wash!

Through our writing lessons, we tried our hands at chants, riddles, simple cinquains, and acrostics. We wrote short poetic statements about memories, holidays, seasons, and dreams. We examined predictable books and modeled books and poems after them. We brought in objects and wrote about them: rusty keys, ragged tennis shoes, and old, chipped, Indian pottery. We took colorful and stimulating pictures from a file and wrote about what we felt while looking at them. Sometimes we listened to music while we wrote. Along the way we stumbled onto our own wonderful combination of words. We pasted these into our writing books or stapled them onto construction paper and made them into poetry books. In our early apprenticeship in wordsmithing, we discovered that there was much to write about and many ways of saying it. We found satisfaction in simply playing with our beginning writing voices.

Along my teaching pathway, I have happened on many fine books that have given me additional ideas. Often they have provided the necessary inspiration for me to teach poetry to my younger students.

I will mention some of my favorites—books that I think should be a part of any primary teacher's professional library.

- *Beyond Words: Writing Poems with Children* by Elizabeth McKim and Judith W. Steinbergh. Written by two poets and teachers, this is a simple and wonderful book on working with children in writing poetry. The authors' examples are clear, and their methods demonstrate how easily children can learn to create moving and original poetry. A fine resource for elementary teachers.
- *Knock at a Star: A Child's Introduction to Poetry* by X. J. Kennedy and Dorothy M. Kennedy. An excellent source of poems and short poetry discussions for younger students. A section at the end of the book offers suggestions to students on writing their own poems.
- *Let Them Write Poetry* by Nina Willis Walter. A beautifully written and conceived book on children and poetry, Walter's book has become a standard text on the subject. She includes examples from children, plus ideas and activities on both writing and appreciation of poetry.
- *Moving Windows: Evaluating the Poetry Children Write* by Jack Collom. From a poet's point of view, Jack Collom talks about the poetry children write. He illustrates his points with numerous examples of poems children have written in his classes. Having had the opportunity to visit Jack while he was working with a class of third graders, I know firsthand how valuable and insightful his comments are.
- *Pass the Poetry, Please* by Lee Bennett Hopkins. A classic text on poetry with sections on both poets and poetry materials presently available. Of particular note is the chapter entitled "Butterflies Can Be in Bellies," in which Hopkins explains many techniques and short poetic forms that can be used when working with young children in writing poetry.
- *The Whole Word Catalogue* edited by Rosellen Brown, Marvin Hoffman, Martin Kushner, Phillip Lopate, and Sheila Murphy, and
- *The Whole Word Catalogue 2*, edited by Bill Zavatsky and Ron Padgett. Although not geared exclusively to any one age group, these two books comprise a storehouse of ideas and activities that can be used in the classroom, kindergarten through high school. *Catalogue 2* is of special interest because it includes some valuable essays by writers who have

been involved in the Teachers and Writers Projects around the country. Both books have much to offer and challenge the classroom teacher.

- *Wishes, Lies and Dreams* by Kenneth Koch. Referred to in some detail in chapter 5, this book is mentioned here again as a solid stepping stone in poetry writing with younger children.

Fairy dust

Referring back to Dorothy Aldis's poem "On a Snowy Day" (page 113) you have to wonder: fence posts wearing hats made of marshmallows, bushes in prayer, and trees dancing in skirts? Where did she get these images? How many billions of people have seen fence posts covered with snow—and seen *only* fence posts covered with snow? Why did the image apparently occur only to Dorothy Aldis? And, while we are wondering, why do some children appear to have such vivid and accessible imaginations, while others, after your best motivational brainstorming session, come up with the grass is like a green doorknob?

I wonder if I could convince you of the possibility of a sprinkle of fairy dust in the eyes of some of our youngsters, a mysterious quality that allows them a particularly imaginative view of the world around them. No? Well, someone far wiser than I could better analyze and explain for you the differences we see in children's creativity. I only know that saying simply, "Okay, kids, be sure to use your imaginations in your poems," is like whispering in the midst of a shouting match.

So how can we foster creativity with our budding wordsmiths (since fairy dust is hard to locate these days)? I suggest that a great deal of the poet's imagination lies in creative observation—not simply seeing an object, but seeing *into* that object; wondering what it feels; describing it by likening it to something else; or using it to see something else. The child poet Hilda Conkling saw a dandelion, as we all have done, but she observed a "little soldier with a golden helmet." William D. Sargent heard a pack of wolves howling in the night, but in his mind saw "wind wolves hunting" across the sky. David McCord must have walked in the summer rain, feeling the water dripping down his body, to say "to walk in warm rain / till you drip like a drain." Poets see the world around them through eyes that transform the world. They see through a "poet's eyes."

In my classroom, I kept a large pair of oversized, plastic eyeglasses that we called the "poet's glasses." They were meant to provide the students with a sense of seeing as a poet might see. When you put on the glasses, we said you magically were able to see the world through a "poet's eyes." Looking through the glasses, you did not merely see a sunset or even a bright yellow sunset; you observed the sun drawing up all his light in a bag and sneaking it over the back side of Pikes Peak (clearly a poet's view from my Colorado Springs classroom window).

Often when talking to a child about what I considered to be an uninspired description in his writing, I would simply suggest that he try on the poet's glasses for size to see if they could help liven up the piece. I encouraged all my young writers to cherish what they saw with their poet's eyes, to train themselves to observe their environment as though they were trying to discover secrets about it.

When viewing the world through a poet's eyes, the children discovered that they must look—really look—at the world around them, using all their senses. Looking around our classroom, I would ask:

What colors do you see?
Shades of colors?
What feelings do you associate
with the colors?

How about shapes?
Any shapes in our room?
Textures?
Patterns?

Rub your mind's hand around the room.
How does it feel?

Close your eyes.
Hear anything?
Listen carefully.

Oh, no—how about smells?
Any smells in our room?

In a learning center, I placed individual objects such as paper clips, selections of fruit, and ornate vases, and pairs of youngsters would practice describing the objects through their senses.

How does the object feel
to the tips of your fingers,

to the end of your tongue,
to the sense of your nose?

Does it make a sound?

What associations do you have with the object?

On butcher paper spread out on the floor, we would brainstorm for specific word images for general nondescriptive words such as *cold* (Figure 6–3) or *hot* (Figure 6–4).

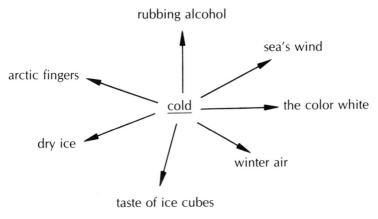

Figure 6–3

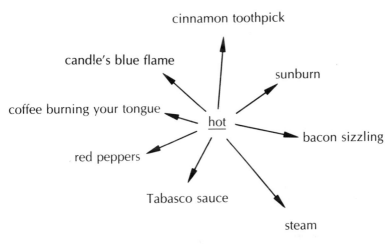

Figure 6–4

Another activity I tried was to fill up a bowl with small strips of paper. On each strip I had written a word or words. For example:

windy evening
moon shadows
fear
town parade
aspen leaf
knotted old tree
mud between toes
cowlick
quarter moon
dawn
tickle
pain

The children would reach into the bowl, fish out a strip, and, working in groups, see who could create the most vivid one-line image:

Fear strikes like cat shrieks in the night.

Comparing the different images, we would discuss what made an image good.

Occasionally I would have imagination warm-up exercises in what I called "three-minute, three-word drills":

Okay, gang, get your paper and pencil—
remember you can only make three-word images and
you have only three minutes.
Today's word: HOME—H . . . O . . . M . . . E. Go!

The kids then would have three minutes to scribble as quickly as they could all the three-word images that came to their minds.

warm at night
creaks in wind
smells of food . . .

and so on.

Activities such as these (and there are literally thousands of them) help put youngsters in touch with what I call their "imaginative selves." They discover that words can weave the magical with the real, the ordinary with the strange, the whimsical with the serious, and the "far-out" with the everyday. By using their own poet's eyes, they come to believe that all of us were in fact born with at least a sprinkle of fairy dust in our eyes.

OLDER KIDS—THE WRITING WORKSHOP

I never knew when it was going to happen; it just did. I'd turn around and there it was again. Maybe it didn't occur until after the Halloween party for the fifth graders, when they'd settled down into a comfortable daily routine; or maybe it was late winter with my third graders, after the last straggling, cursive capital letter was finally mastered. Or sometimes it could happen relatively early in the year with my seventh graders when my classroom management strategies miraculously jelled and the class and I began to function as learning partners. But each year, without warning or fanfare, my writing classes slowly changed into writing workshops. The change didn't occur at the same time each year—some years it was earlier and some years, later. Some classes had me convinced that it would never happen and nearly proved me right. But somewhere between "Welcome to my class" and "Have a nice summer" the whole behavior and routine surrounding my writing instruction metamorphosized and like a butterfly emerging—a new creature, from its restrictive, hard cocoon shell—I found the students successfully learning about writing in a workshop atmosphere.

How did I know that what I was seeing was no longer writing class but a workshop? It's hard to say exactly—it's as much a feeling as anything else. If I had to describe a workshop in one sentence, I would say that a writing workshop exists when the students work in a structured classroom routine that allows them to behave as writers learning about writing individually through the practice of many forms of writing. Forgive me—much too general a statement, I know; I always hated that in my college method textbooks. But I told you it was a feeling. Perhaps I finally had a workshop when I noticed that the questions and comments the students were making began to sound like those of practicing writers: "This line just doesn't seem to work," or "Oh, boy, I know I lost the reader here," as opposed to "How many pages do I have to fill up?" or "Do we have to spell all the words correctly?" Maybe it was when I suddenly found myself spending more of my time sitting alongside kids as a writing coach instead of in front of the class giving directions. I'm not exactly sure how or why with each class, but I knew when it had changed.

Perhaps I could compare the behavior of a writing class and a writing workshop:

In a writing class...

I select our one weekly writing topic and form.

All the children are always involved in the same activity at the same time (listening, drafting, correcting).

All the children are always writing on the same given assignment.

When the children complete an assignment they bring it to me at my desk.

The majority of the class time is spent with me explaining things.

In a writing workshop...

The children generate many of their own topics and make decisions about what form they want to use.

The students may be at different points in their writing (some are paired up talking; some are intensely writing by themselves; some are in conference with a group; some are at an editing center; some are illustrating; some are daydreaming).

At different times, the children have three or four (or possibly more) writing drafts going. Some are finishing a mini-science report, and some, a biography; some are grappling with a new poem.

I'm not to be found at my desk—I may be writing, or talking to a circle of students, or I may be daydreaming. The students have folders in which they keep their writing.

The majority of time is spent with the children involved in writing and writing activities.

In a writing class...	**In a writing workshop...**
I refer to the students as "students."	I refer to the students as "authors" and "poets" and "fine wordsmiths."
All the desks are in neat lines, facing—guess who—me!	The room is arranged to accommodate many writing activities—silent writing, pairing, critics' circle, listening area, and illustration table.
By and large I'm the only one who makes comments on a child's writing.	The children interact with each other's writing frequently. There is a special wooden stool where they sit when they read their pieces to a group.
My comments are about a child's writing and are geared toward improving that one particular piece that day.	*Our* comments are geared toward solving writing problems in general so children may use the comments and advice another day in another piece of writing.

When my writing classes did evolve into workshops, I found the situation vacillating between being a terribly relaxing time during which my students quietly went about the business of becoming more knowledgeable, confident writers and a more frenzied time as a "short order cook" facing constant demands: "Need a B.L.T.—hold the mayo—right away." "Where's the writing paper?" "Who's going to conference me?" "I can't find my writing folder." In any case, the workshop atmosphere was a joy because it gave me the opportunity to see language learning at its peak as well as rare glimpses of youngsters learning with each other while making one discovery after another about themselves as writers.

Understandably, since a thorough examination of the writing process and writing workshops is well beyond the limited scope of this book, I'll only mention that there is a proliferation of fine books coming out now on the subject. Donald Graves, Lucy McCormick Calkins, and Peter Elbow are just a few writers and researchers who are making great headway on what we know about how children become writers. I encourage you to become familiar with their research and insights.

I mention the writing workshop because it was within the structure and routine of a workshop that my students eventually made the greatest gains not only as poets but also as writers of stories and reports and essays. It was into the workshop with the younger kids that I brought pattern books and model poems for their early forays into writing poetry; and it was in the workshop that I shared word exercises with older kids to sharpen and tune up their wordsmithing skills and used pieces of literature from which the youngsters could learn about the poet's craft. It was within the setting of the workshop that I could individually coach kids on the poetry they had written, and that they could critique and honor each other's work and begin behaving like poets selecting their own topics and making crucial decisions about their work. Most importantly, it was in the workshop that I got to learn alongside the children.

Readying the soil

Although I never knew exactly when my writing classes were going to mature into true writing workshops, I knew I had quite consciously been "readying the soil" and preparing the students. I knew that if, for example, I eventually wanted my students to generate their own writing topics, I had to give them strategies for collecting and developing writing ideas. "Write-about-whatever-turns-you-on" went out with love beads and sandals. If I wanted them to attain proficiency at revising and editing their own work, I had to teach them, at some point, step-by-step editing skills and to design activities and procedures so that they could practice these skills. If I wanted them to become involved in productive peer conferencing and critique groups, I had to model and demonstrate those types of behaviors myself long before they were to occur in my workshop setting.

The same is true for wordsmithing skills. If I wished the students to become conscious of precise word choices and the use of concrete, sensory details in their poems, I had to gradually introduce lessons that facilitated the acquisition of those attitudes and skills. It was essential to involve students in language experiences and classroom activities that encouraged their understanding of the power of images if I ever wanted them to attempt to use images in their own writing. If I hoped they would be comfortable with the use of metaphors by the spring, I had

to allow them time to come to discover the beauty of metaphoric language during the fall.

Nothing of lasting value in language arts is learned overnight. It
takes time. It takes time for students to develop a friendly working
relationship between their thoughts and their writing. It takes time
for them to come to trust their writing voices. I suspect it takes
nothing short of a lifetime for poets to completely recognize and
control their own poetic voices. To the student writer, therefore,
the writing process will always be more valuable than the written
product.

I have been asked innumerable times to come to a school for
a day to "teach the kids to write poetry." What a request! I
could no more do that in a day than I could cultivate a lush,
botanic garden from a Kansas prairie in one August afternoon.
Any good gardener knows that readying and preparing the soil
takes a lot of work, if seeds—even the most expensive seeds—
are to grow and thrive and become award-winning plants. So,
too, with our students.

I am reminded of poets-in-the-schools programs, often graciously
funded by local and national arts and humanities councils, in which
very fine poets and writers blitz a classroom with lively writing
sessions a couple of times a week for two to three weeks and then
leave. Although I applaud the idea that students get to meet "real"
poets face-to-face, and I am aware of the unique and varied teaching
techniques that have evolved out of such programs, I am skeptical
of the "hit-and-run" nature of programs such as these. Myra Cohn
Livingston, in her excellent and extensively researched text, *The
Child as Poet: Myth or Reality*, says clearly:

> It takes time to learn that poetry is not a message where the
> reader is told how to feel and behave; not a greeting card or a
> commercial, badly rhymed doggerel, a series of quick discon-
> nected images, nor a recorded experience. (Livingston 1984,
> 274)

A couple of poetic shots in the arm a couple of times a week for
only a few weeks is simply not enough time. Think how much more
beneficial my visit or another poet's residency would be to the
students if they had been given the opportunity throughout the year
to read and react to a lot of different poetry, if they had begun to
develop a feel and an "ear" for poetic language, and if they had
been writing their own poems and gaining personal practice in the
craft of wordsmithing.

Hoping eventually to foster confident, creative wordsmiths, I often spent the early part of the year "preparing the soil" by, of course, sharing many poems with my students. In addition to our discussion and the many activities I ordinarily use with poetry, I maintained a Poetry Center in the classroom. This center included numerous books of poetry (both anthologies and individual picture books); cassette tapes, records, poetry filmstrips; and a series of poetry activity sheets. For this purpose, Lee Bennett Hopkins's book, *Pass the Poetry, Please,* has the most thorough listing of poetry materials currently available. For primary and intermediate teachers, Bill Martin Jr's recent *Treasure Chest of Poetry* is an outstanding resource for poems, inspiration, and ideas. For your Poetry Center, I refer you to both of these items, as well as to the ideas and suggestions included throughout this book.

In conjunction with this immersion of my students in the world of poetry, my "readying the soil" included the ongoing use of the poetry notebooks previously mentioned. The notebooks, you will recall, were a gathering of class poems, individual selections, favorite images, reaction sheets, and an assortment of what I called word tinkerings—simple word-play activities (I've mentioned a few of these and will mention more).

Becoming comfortable with poetry as an art form is an obvious first step in the writing process and not one that can be hurried or forced. It is the basic literary groundwork that must be laid before students can be expected to experience much success or satisfaction writing this thing called "poetry."

Levels of language

In addition to helping my students become more comfortable with poetry itself, I also assisted them to see poetry within the broader circumference of writing in general. My goal was to have them see that written language was not merely *one* thing—rather, poetic language was *one* of the different ways in which words could be used to express a writer's thoughts and ideas. Like the villagers in my story, they needed to realize that, depending on the author's purpose, there were different levels of usage in language. One level was neither better nor worse than another; in fact, the levels often overlapped. Each employed a different intention and use of words. I presented a model of different levels of language (see Figure 6–5), adapted from the one in *Sounds of Language Reading Series* (Martin 1975).

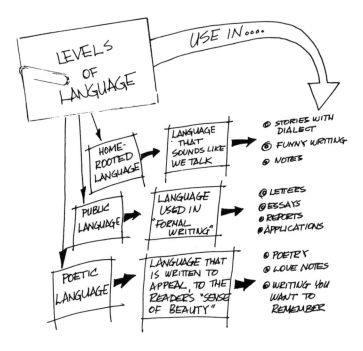

Figure 6–5

Home-rooted language, I told the students, was the "gift of their homes." It was the language they spoke, learned from their parents and home environment. "It's a wonderfully rich and uniquely expressive language," I told them. I stressed that home-rooted language was not a "wrong" language just because it was, at times, grammatically incorrect. It was one of several forms of language—the one tied closest to our learning to speak. It was the language that tried to reproduce the sounds of everyday people going about their everyday lives. As an illustration, I used James Whitcomb Riley's home-rooted verse, which voiced the expressions and pronunciations of rural Indiana people:

> O the Raggedy Man! He works for Pa;
> An' he's the goodest man ever you saw!
> He comes to our house every day,
> An' waters the horses, an' feeds 'em hay.
>
> (JAMES WHITCOMB RILEY, "The Raggedy Man")

Another use of language is public language. Public language is the language of conventions, of rules, and of correctness. It is the language modern society developed over the centuries to conduct the business and ceremonies of public life. It is a language based on strict adherence to rules of usage. I always told my students that it was important not only to know the difference between home-rooted and public language, but also when to use each one. The King's English, articulated by a nine-year-old character in a children's story, seems as inappropriate as home-rooted expressions on a job application or on a document in a courtroom.

Finally, there is poetic language—language that is written to last, to appeal to a reader's innate sense of beauty. Like the wordsmith in my story who tried to make his words stick in the minds and hearts of the villagers, those who attempt to use poetic language are trying to arrange their thoughts, their words, in the most memorable way. As I have mentioned before, this level of language is "the best words in the best order."

As a class project a university student of mine showed her fourth graders how public language could be redrafted as poetic language. She worked with them on a prose piece one of them had written:

WHO WANTS A CHEAP DRAGON?
Hey kids, I have a dragon for sale,
really cheap. There are lots of things
you can do with a dragon. For instance,
you could hire him as a heater. He could
heat you up on a cold snowy day. If you
have firewood, but no match, you could
pay him to make a fire.

The class transformed it to:

DRAGONS

Dragons for sale
Dragons for pay
Heat you up
On a snowy day.

Dragons for sale
Dragons for hire
Use for a match
If you need a fire.

A similar change is reflected here:

GIRAFFE

> There are lots of things you
> can do with a giraffe. For
> instance, you can use it for a
> slide, or to ride on, or
> do lots of tricks on.

GIRAFFE

> *A giraffe*
> *A giraffe*

S
  l
    i
      d
        e

          o
           n

R
  i
    d
      e

        o
         n

Do lots of

t
  r
    i
      c
       k
      s

        o
         n.

Having students recognize the differences between levels of language in their reading material and identify when different levels are being used and when they overlap, encourages students as practicing writers to become more aware of the resources of language. For as they begin to make decisions about their writing and the suitable level of language they need to capture what it is they want to say, they begin to internalize the behavior of writers. Most importantly, they start to adjust their writing according to its purpose and audience. My own master's thesis, for example, found its most authentic voice as public language; my most memorable short writings are poems; and my most popular story tried for months to be a poem, but as time went by, revealed itself to be a home-rooted prose story.

Writing folders

As my older students began to perceive language as malleable and to understand that they, as writers, decide how to mold it and give it shape according to their topic and purpose, they started to develop writing folders to use in our workshops. These were folders in which they kept their rough drafts, not only of poetry but also of stories, articles, and other writings. In addition, their folders contained rough sketches of possible future writings, critique comments, on-going written assignments from other subject areas, and whatever they needed in the writing workshop. Inside each folder, on the left side, was stapled a sheet entitled, "What Should I Write About?" with three categories: *Things I Know a Lot About, Story Ideas*, and *Wonderings?* (see Figure 6–6). It was here that my students started to do their own gathering of possible writing topics.

Attached to the right side of the folder was another sheet: "What I've Written About" (see Figure 6–7). Here the students recorded the progress of their writing with titles, completion dates, and information on whether the piece had been group critiqued, the person with whom they had had a conference, and finally, the date the piece had been published or completed. This portion of the folder was particularly helpful to me during writing conferences with the student as well as parent/teacher conferences, because it represented evidence as to the effort and amount of work being accomplished by the student.

It is my belief that no substantial growth in a student's writing will occur, in any genre, until there is some personal investment—

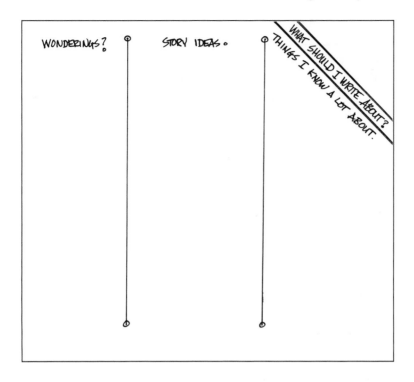

Figure 6–6

until the student begins writing about topics that mean something to her, personal happenings she wants to recount, or ideas that intrigue her. The writing folders allowed my students to keep an ongoing list of those types of concerns. In the folders, they recorded those things about which they knew a lot and felt themselves to be experts. They were constantly on the lookout for ideas and happenings that could be developed into a story or poem. And finally, they collected subjects and ideas about which they had questions.

Occasionally I would give them a topic assignment. For example, I might have them list as many "changes" as they could think of (child to adult, day to night, negative attitude to positive attitude, etc.). We would compile a class list, and the students would choose the ones that most intrigued them and add these to their writing folders. In other subject areas during the day we would discover possible writing topics we could add to our folders as they occurred.

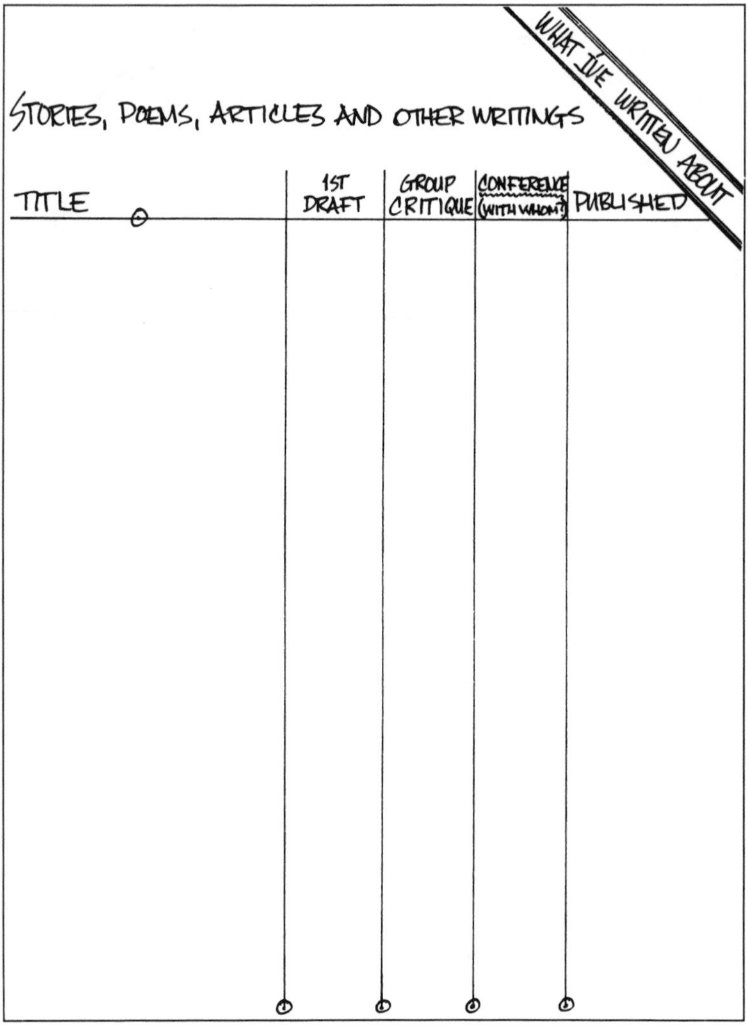

STORIES, POEMS, ARTICLES AND OTHER WRITINGS	WHAT I'VE WRITTEN ABOUT			
TITLE	1ST DRAFT	GROUP CRITIQUE	CONFERENCE (WITH WHOM)	PUBLISHED

Figure 6–7

Or with the poems we were reading we would find interesting ideas to explore with our own words. These lists were the catalysts for students to discover that *Star Wars*—or the latest movie craze—wasn't the only story that needed to be written and that "love" and "flowers" were not the only topics that they could mold into poetry. They could discover greater satisfaction when they wrote about things of importance to them: changes in their personal lives, wild fantasies, fears, dreams, intriguing people, places (both real and invented), and recalled events. As writers and poets, they were restricted only by what they failed to notice in the world around them and by the limits of their imaginations.

The curse

For many years, I have used both the concept of the levels of language and writing folders with a variety of age groups. I have come to believe that there is a writing *curse* that descends when students cross the line from home-rooted and/or public language into poetic language. I have observed that a mere six words, either spoken aloud or thought, may have a devastating effect on the writing of students. The words, "I'M GOING TO WRITE A POEM," are like some ancient, mysterious spell. They turn some students formerly capable of strong, forceful writing, into weak, syrupy writers. Some students suddenly try to cram archaic words like *t'was* or *ne'er* into their writing, while others search high and low for the most trite rhymes for the most common of words. Such seems to be the supernatural power of these six words.

For whatever reason, the thought of writing a poem has always drastically lowered the level of my students' writing. Suddenly they forget that, since September, I have stressed that we write about things and ideas that are important and interesting to us. They seem completely unable to recall my hammering away at the idea that good writing is a result of using concrete nouns and vivid verbs. They begin loading up their poems with the vaguest of adjectives—

I like the gay play
of blue ways
in wonderful summer days—

and with the most overused images and rhymes known to the human ear:

I like Spring
because it brings
flowerings.

It almost seems that, as if under some strange spell, when my students venture into the realm of poetic language all the good writing growth I have come to enjoy in them vanishes.

To counteract the curse, I developed a verbal chart in my classroom. It was called "Mr. D's Three C's for Writing Poetry." It was written on the board; it became a class saying; it was glued onto a corner of the writing folders; and it was chorused back and forth more times than should have been required of anyone. (One former student swears I made her write it twenty-five times for punishment for rhyming "true" with "blue" for what was surely the nine-hundredth time.) I can only imagine how many of my former students hear the echo of these words now if they sit down to write a poem:

MR. D's

THREE C's

FOR WRITING POETRY:

  1. Create images.
  2. Convey feelings.
  3. Communicate through associations.

The chant expresses in its simplest form what I considered essential to their poetry writing. First, they needed to use images—fresh, original images of their own making. If a poem had nothing else but a striking image or two, then it was worth the effort. Second, their poems needed to contain some degree of sincerity on the part of the authors. They had to care enough or empathize enough with their poems' subjects for the pieces to have integrity. Finally, each poem had to connect with the reader by means of association, and often this was through the use of the "metaphoric dimension," if the poem was to be meaningful.

It is my hope that this chant, similarly used, might help other students escape the curse and move into the world of poetic language with the best of their writing ideas and skills intact.

Word tinkerings—finger exercises for wordsmithing

I must confess that, in spite of my verbal antidote, my students were not completely free of the "I'm-going-to-write-a-poem" curse. I found they also needed to have some hands-on experience with actual wordsmithing skills. The experience came in exercises I called "word tinkerings." Word tinkerings were activities that allowed the students to play around with words and ideas in poetry (oftentimes free of the anxiety of having to end up with a product, a POEM). In a sense, these exercises coerced students to push the language around and to see what they could discover in the words they used.

I have found word tinkering to be a particularly valuable experience for older students, because they are so often stalled at a "safety plateau" in their writing. In or around third grade, students have command of safe, controlled, no-error sentences:

Subject. Predicate. End mark.

No chance for mistakes. No word play. No experimentation. No imagination.

Clearly, students found comfort in the fact that these easily formulated, mistake-free sentences kept their papers clean of any red marks and were well-received by their teachers. The problem, of course, was that their writing began to sound like pages from workbooks and examples from skill sheets:

Bill came to my house. We had
cookies. It was fun.

The spontaneous writing they had created a few years before had ceased. Their innocent juxtaposition of words and thoughts and their innate delight in word play had been lost to the god COR-RECTNESS. And, as weak as it made their prose, it all but slammed the door on their poetic endeavors. Their poetry resembled poetic workbook pages, paragraphs revamped to look like poetry:

WINTER

I like the winter.
It's nice and snowy.
Do you like the winter?

The "three C's" for writing poetry (create images, convey feelings, communicate through associations) could not be achieved within the bounds of "subject, predicate, end mark." The students needed to experiment, to take chances, to feel comfortable "pushing" the language around to see what they could create. They needed, at times, to break all the rules, until they found surprises within the language.

In hopes of helping students leap off their safety plateaus, I included in my writing workshops word-tinkering exercises designed to encourage students to "mix-it-up" with words: to discover how the juxtaposition of a couple of ordinary words could create an out-of-the-ordinary image; to see how a natural speaking rhythm could be induced by the rearrangement of the words in a line; or to experiment with the different effects that line breaks could have on their work. I wanted them to discover how similar sounds playing off each other could be the kickoff for a very memorable line. Word tinkerings were used, therefore, to facilitate those types of discoveries. This learning, I hoped, would then dribble slowly, like a creamy chocolate sauce, onto their actual poetry writing.

Basic word tinkering—all poetic efforts, for that matter—began with a degree of word play, or a shuffling around of words, ideas, and thoughts to see what struck a true note. By playing with words, my students' attention was drawn to specific words and word patterns, to surprising and powerful word combinations and arrangements. To start, I kept a large plastic Ziploc freezer bag filled with numerous words printed on small strips of tag board. These included examples of vivid words, concrete words, sensory words, and words that evoked a picture in one's mind—words like *starfish* and *moonlight, hawk* and *silver, prickly* and *dazzle.*

From time to time, students would take a handful of the words, spread them out on the floor in a corner of the room, and begin randomly to arrange and rearrange them. Like a piano player tinkering with random notes and musical chords, a child would pair up curious words and groups of words until something startled him. I like "crimson starlight," one would say. Or "dusk of day." "A slithering, snickering snake" would be mischievously blurted across the room.

The students could trade their words with others or reach back into the plastic bag for another handful. While they played they could add words of their own or connecting words such as articles and prepositions to form phrases. They wrote their favorite images and phrases in their poetry notebooks. Here's a sampling of what their playing found:

whistle cranberry cricket
wrinkled old lies
misty dusk dreams
sticky barefoot stench
violet rainbow feather kisses
pussy willow pleasures

I developed an extension of this activity after watching Jack Collom (author of *Moving Windows: Evaluating the Poetry Children Write*) working with a class of third graders. He would have the children work in pairs and write "lunes" (Collom 1985, 3). The "lune" is a simplification of the haiku, in which the students count words instead of syllables. These lunes would have three lines, of three words, five words, and three words, consecutively. Jack would have one of the students write the first line (three words) and give it to his partner, who would write the second line (five words) and return it to the first person for the last line (three words). Here's an example from the school where I observed him:

Picture my cat
Shedding all over the house
and me sneezing.

Borrowing Jack's technique, I would have my students get the first line of the lune by taking one of the three-word phrases they discovered on the floor with words from the word bag and then doing the same thing—passing the developing poem back and forth. The second and third lines were composed by the students without words from the word bag. Here are a couple of my students' examples:

snakeskin soil smoke
in the great big countryside
that eagles smell

fierce creepy spiders
crawl on dawn's day coming—
gives me the creeps

"React to the words you hear with words you feel," I told them. "Free your minds to learn how to react with words. Don't let meaning get in the way. Have fun. Be on the lookout for word surprises."

As the year moved on, our word bag grew because we kept adding words that we found in our reading. The surprising beauty and power of the images the students discovered was what I wanted them to strive toward in their own writing endeavors. I wanted them always to keep in mind the idea that certain words can evoke more than others. To reinforce this, I kept an ongoing chart on my bulletin board of strong and weak images from their writing:

Concrete word images	*Vague, boring, and overused word images*
peanut butter brown	blue sky
fire breath	happy day

Concrete word images	Vague, boring, and overused word images
blush of raspberry	sweet as a rose
a musty dust cough	slow as a turtle

Another word-tinkering exercise was to take a topic such as "student," "principal," "puppy," or whatever, and create "hyphenated-images" describing the topic. Figure 6–8 shows an example using the subject "puppy." Also from the exercise, here's a "hyphenated poem" about video games, written by a sixth grader:

VIDEO GAMES

> *crackle-poppings*
> *thumbs-gyrating*
> *minds-jerking*
> *eyeballs-darting*
> *quarters-going*

In the same way I encouraged them to play with odd combinations of words to find new images. I had them experiment with an arrangement of words to create a musical line or one that simply "sounded good"—a line they could almost sing. Each month I would give them a list of twenty-five random words and ask if they could use their "ears" to see if they could strike a chord with the words. They could only add articles and suffixes. Again, I didn't have them concern themselves with meaning.

Here is one month's list:

bitter	lonely
mist	whisper
leap	bare

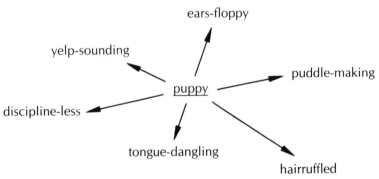

Figure 6–8

silver	snow
wail	wild
willow	far
chill	gloss
cozy	slice
swift	whistle
five	wing
wind	moon
dim	golden
wove	

And, here, some of their finds:

the fine mist woven of golden silk

a swift leap over the bare snow

the wild chill wove through the wind

the dim mist whispered silver snow

I would have them take their lines and play with different designs:

the fine mist
woven
of golden silk

or

the fine
mist
woven
of golden
silk

or

the fine
mist woven
of
golden silk

I asked them which one appealed to them. Which brought the music of the words to the reader's ears? I told them to notice how a word at the end of a line lingers momentarily on the reader's mind.

I designed other word tinkerings to help students become acquainted with the free use of metaphoric language. A beginning exercise I often used was to have students write what I called "body-likes,'' in which they would compare parts of their bodies to other things. Here are some of these:

> *my hands are muscle-vices that grip*
> *a baseball bat*

> *my legs are like balancing sticks*
> *with tennis shoes*

> *my hair is thousands of skinny, curving pencil lines*

> *my tongue is a fish hiding*
> *in a dark cave*

A similar exercise used their emotions:

> *when I'm angry I'm a bag of*
> *punches*

> *when I'm happy I'm the beginning*
> *of a movie—after the credits*

> *when I'm lonely I'm the last*
> *tear dried before falling asleep*

I encouraged the kids to find metaphors or similes that would catch readers off-guard—something that they might never have heard before.

Metaphoric language can also be used to describe a place. I invented and used a game in which students would describe a place they knew only with similes and have the class try to guess what place was being described. Each line had to begin with the word "like" and, of course, their lines couldn't give away the name of the place:

?

like a rusty bicycle
like spider webs
like a cold cement floor
like scattered tools
like old recapped cans of paint
like pepperings of rat evidence
like dust and mildew
like spots and pools of oil

Did you guess that it was a garage?

An exciting use of metaphoric language was accomplished with the interjection of senses not normally used to describe a particular idea. Instead of writing "Anger feels like *me and my brother fighting,*" we would say something like "Anger tastes like *hot sauce all over you.*" Sentences to be completed, such as "Blue-green smells like _____"; or "Silence sounds like _____"; or "Time looks like _____" were word tinkering exercises that students could work on to discover alternative ways of expressing an idea.

Through word tinkering exercises such as these, my students gained hands-on experience with some of the wordsmithing craft. They learned that as poets they needed to be on the lookout for the unexpected and to sensitize their ears to the sounds, rhythms, and flow of words. These activities awakened in them an appreciation of the power of word pictures and gave them alternatives to the trite and overused. They learned through word tinkering that there are no necessarily bad words—only more successful words.

The word tinkerings I have mentioned in this section are only the shy tip, a hint, of the numerous activities and word games that can be used in your classrooms to release poetry from your unsuspecting students. Add to that the countless other writing ideas and poetic forms that can be introduced, and you will discover that there is more than enough material for a lifetime of teaching. As with the books I found helpful as a primary teacher, there are many insightful books available for teachers who work with older kids. I will highlight some of those that I have found particularly useful through the years.

- *The Art of Teaching Writing* by Lucy McCormick Calkins. Destined to become the writing text classic, *The Art of Teaching Writing* should be required reading for all teachers. Of particular interest to teachers of poetry writing is Calkins's chapter entitled "Poetry." This is a stimulating discussion of how what we know as the "writing process" can include poetry writing.
- *For Poets* by Stephen Dunning, M. Joe Eaton, and Malcolm Glass. Originally part of a Scholastic Series, this book is a collection of what I would call "word tinkerings," guaranteed to stimulate a greater word awareness and facility with intermediate to older students. The book contains many fine ideas, cleverly conceived.
- *Getting from Here to There: Writing and Reading Poetry* by

Florence Grossman. A fine book for teachers of junior high students, this poetry writing anthology presents examples of poems and related writing ideas. Each chapter focuses on and illustrates a different poetic technique with concrete suggestions to help the students follow up by creating their own poems afterwards.

- *The Poetry Connection* by Nina Nyhart and Kinereth Gensler; *Sleeping on the Wing* by Kenneth Koch and Kate Farrell; *Rose, Where Did You Get That Red?* by Kenneth Koch. These three excellent books use the reading of poems by great (and not so great) poets to trigger poetry writing in students. I referred to this writing strategy in chapter 5.
- *The Poetry Writing Handbook* by Neil Baldwin. This excellent step-by-step approach uses an understanding of a contemporary poem to stimulate a follow-up writing exercise. Each chapter is built around a thematic unit. The book is very usable in intermediate to junior high classrooms.
- *Writing Incredibly Short Plays, Poems, Stories* by James H. Norton and Frances Gretton. This book's middle section on writing incredibly short poems may be one of the most practical on the subject. If you can find this book, hold on to it!

GAINING INDEPENDENCE—WRITING STRATEGIES

As I look back on my years of teaching, I have decided that my poetry writing instruction was like my learning to ride a two-wheeler. My bike and I generally kept going forward, but inevitably I tilted and fell to one side or the other. On one side, my instruction revolved around mostly poetic gimmickry—word games, pattern books, model poems, and many of the tinkerings I have described in previous sections, which can also be found in many other books on the market. Tilting to the other side, my instruction was more like standing apart and letting students take much of the initiative and control in their writing. In my writing workshops they found their own stimulation and motivation; they discovered ways to direct their own writing progress. I merely coached. Each successive year was different. Some years, for whatever reason, the students were highly independent and did not need all the gimmickry to produce poetry. Other years, they needed a great deal of it just to eke out one poem.

I suspect that my best poetry instruction was similar to my most triumphant times on my shiny red bicycle, those times when I miraculously circled the block without falling once, all the time keeping my balance. In the classroom, I was at my best when I discovered how much directed classroom activity and how much independence were necessary for students to gain the confidence to explore their own lives with words. It is finding this balance that I recommend as a teaching goal to all poetry teachers. As much success as I found using all the poetry activities, I still knew that the greatest gains in students' writing would occur only when they began to perceive themselves as independent writers in charge of their own writing growth. I therefore used word tinkerings, but I was always working toward helping students invest in and take control of their own learning. I used and created games that facilitated language discoveries by students, but I also placed them in a structure from which they might venture comfortably out on their own as writers. I tried to discern how much string to let out, so that they might soar freely like kites on their own—but without getting tangled in telephone wires.

In my experience, the major problem most (if not all) students face in taking an idea from their writing folders and developing it successfully as a poem on their own (other than the fatal word curse, of course) was that they lacked an accessible and workable poetry writing strategy. They had worked successfully on their own in other genres with other writing strategies. In writing stories, for example, they knew how to develop a sequence sheet outlining the occurrence of events in their stories. They had internalized questions to ask themselves as they wrote: Where will the characters be introduced? What is the problem or conflict in the story? How will it be resolved? Have I created a setting in which the story can happen? And so forth. Their stories grew from this process.

Also, when writing a research report, they knew how to outline and categorize their information first by breaking it into topics. They then sequenced the topics into paragraphs. They knew how to develop their topic paragraphs and how to include an introductory paragraph and conclude with a concise summary of their ideas. None of these strategies, however, could be used with this thing called "poetry."

Lacking a workable writing strategy, many students follow what I call a "title down" process. They write the subject of their poem as a title, underline it, and start listing everything they can think of about it. Occasionally, they will leave out articles and conjunctions to make the piece appear more like a poem. They end up rambling, with no clear direction.

I LIKE FALL

> *Fall is a very neat time,*
> *The air is a crispy blue*
> *And all the town folks around should like fall*
> *Even those who cannot be found*
> *They must enjoy it for I can't deny it*
> *And Fall, my dear folks, is neat.*

What happens with a "title down" process is that students end up reacting only to a title and not to the experience that originally motivated the writing. Nor in the process do they turn their attention to the music and imagery of the language they are using. When they run out of things to say about the title, they start making up things or repeating themselves.

I encouraged my older students to try a different strategy, one that allowed them to react to the initial experience by casting word images and using personal associations to capture their feelings about their subjects (remember Mr. D's three C's). I wanted them to react with words to the experience. To explain the writing strategy I used, let me first walk you through a process.

As I write today, my beautiful, white-haired, ninety-year-old grandmother lies nearly completely paralyzed from a stroke in a nursing home. When my family visits her, we must gently turn her head to face us and physically cup her frail hand around our index fingers. Her only response to our voices is an occasional, ever-so-light gripping with that hand. Needless to say, we love her dearly and are deeply saddened by her condition. Now, here is an emotional experience, if there ever was one, that I am absorbing, possibly to frame as a poem. I am sure anyone who has had a similar experience has known the same urge to find the words to articulate what he or she felt.

If I were to employ the "title down" process used by students, I would probably begin with a title, "Grandma in a Nursing Home," and start listing thoughts and responding to my title:

GRANDMA IN A NURSING HOME

> *I'm sad*
> *To see my grandmother*

So fragile
Paralyzed
Her fingers are frail

. . . and so on.

But, since I want to re-create what I am feeling for the reader, I need to find strong images and personal associations that capture in words what those feelings are. I need to use the fact that my grandmother is in a nursing home only as a "triggering experience," to use the late poet Richard Hugo's term, and push the poem out from there (Hugo 1979, 5). I need to react in words to the experience and look for associations that might serve the poetic product.

Using what I call a poetic triggering sheet (see Figure 6–9), I can

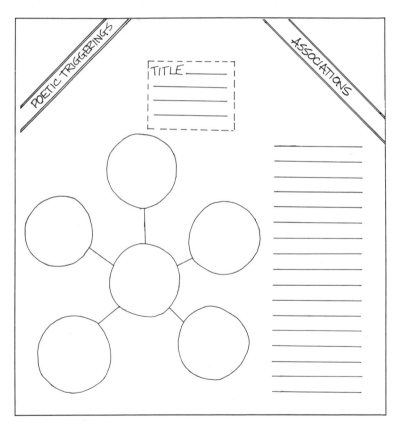

Figure 6–9

put the triggering experience (Grandmother in a nursing home) in the center circle and begin searching for word images. All of a sudden, the words "finger hugs" come to me. They suggest the affection I felt when my grandmother gripped my fingers. I write "finger hugs" in one of the outside circles. From there I recall how parents and grandparents hold up their index fingers and have babies wrap their tiny hands around them. How affectionate a gesture this is. As a baby, I wrapped my hand around my grandmother's; now it is her turn to have her hand wrapped around mine. I write "cycles of affection" in another circle and describe the experience in the lines labeled "Associations." I also respond to my choice of the word "cycle" because it plays off the fact that my grandmother's hand cycles or encircles itself around mine. It also hints at the cycles of life. I like that! I continue looking for word images and associations, which I record on the poetic triggerings sheet, and which may or may not eventually find their way into the poem. It is from this sheet that I pull my raw language materials. From these materials I can begin to apply my wordsmithing skills to see if in fact a poem will emerge.

During the process I think of a "working" title, one that I may want to use or redraft later on. "Touch of Years." I write it in the box surrounded by the dotted line. I remind myself not to be firmly boxed in by this title, but to continue to respond to the experience with words and to try to find the right arrangement of those words with the hope of creating good lines. The title will take care of itself.

In my writing workshops, I make these poetic triggering sheets available as strategy sheets for the students. On their sheets, in the center circle, they put their initiating or triggering experiences (often these experiences come from lists in their writing folders) and then try to find word images that go along with those experiences, which they write in the circles at the ends of the spokes. Just as I did in the word tinkering exercise with "lunes," I encourage them to "react with words" rather than just to describe—to trust themselves to find startling, new images, and not to rely on safe, overused images. I also insist that students try to connect with the reader by using their own personal associations with the experience. Does the experience remind them of something? Can they make an association with the experience by likening it to another or by using it to see or understand something else? Can they put on the poet's glasses and see it through their "poet's eyes"? Students record these types of responses in the column next to the circles. They may want to assign a working title to the piece and write it in the box.

With this process, then, students have the raw material (words and associations) needed to begin wordsmithing—elaborating, or pushing the language around—to see if a poem will emerge. I tell them to remember that the triggering experience should always set off their word imaginations. I remind them that they, like the wordsmith in my story, need not be strictly bound by "actuality." The truth of the poem is in the music and the magic of the statement. What sounds good as an image or word combination in a poem will always be more important than what exactly happened. Unfortunately, students will also have to discover that not every experience will produce a poem for them, but that they will never know for sure until they try it. They will need to find out that not every idea in their writing folders will take wings as poetry. Some may become stories or some may not be strong enough experiences to trigger the imagination. As they learn this lesson, they will also find out something extremely valuable—that every writing excursion will give them a closer kinship with the composition process and the eventual discovery of their own writing process.

HOBNOBBING WITH THE POETS

For poetry writing students, following a writing strategy provides another valuable linguistic link, beyond comfortable stepping stones, into more independent and self-directed writing. It allows students an insider's view into the poetry of others. Let me explain.

Since I have left teaching in public schools, a portion of my time these days is spent giving speeches or presentations to a variety of groups—reading conferences, teachers' inservices, parent involvement groups. I thoroughly enjoy this part of my work. I like the creativity involved in deciding which poems or stories might be the most appropriate. I enjoy thinking through how I might use these poems and stories within the context of my talk. I like outlining the flow of the points I want to make and rehearsing the actual presentation. The only problem is that, since I've begun this type of work, I find I cannot listen to others' presentations in the same fashion as I did before I began public speaking.

For example, in church, as I sit and listen to the minister, I am analyzing how he makes his transitions from point to point. I am admiring how he ties his selections of scripture into his theme. I am wondering where he got the idea for this illustration or that anecdote. At times, I wonder if I am the only one in the entire congregation noticing what I am noticing. In a sense, I am enjoying his sermon with an insider's view of public speaking. Being a practicing speaker, I am privy to the ins and outs of public speaking customs, and I listen with that knowledge.

I am sure that professional football players watch a football game with the same insider's view. They see and analyze aspects of the game that a "lay person" misses.

This phenomenon occurs in the classroom when children view themselves as insiders in the world of writing. When they begin to make connections between their writing process and the process professional writers must go through, they too are privy to an insider's view. Lucy McCormick Calkins says:

> The reading-writing connections that matter most are the small "ah-has" that happen when a youngster sees glimpses of the relatedness between reading and writing. They are the times when youngsters look up from their writing and suddenly recall another author who has struggled with similar issues. They are the moments of connectedness that a child experiences because he or she is an insider in the world of written language. (Calkins 1986, 232)

With poetry, the "ah-has" and the "reading-writing connections" students make occur when they read poetry through the eyes of a practicing poet. Just as I noticed the craft behind my minister's sermon, they view poems by others in light of their own poetry writing efforts. They notice the effect certain word choices have on the poem's images; they see how breaking a line in a certain place is much more effective than somewhere else; they are silently nodding their heads as they realize how well the poet uses associations, and they wonder how he or she came up with them. In a sense, they are mentally hobnobbing with all poets . . . at the same literary country club:

> *"Yes, Mr. Shakespeare," they say, "I, myself,*
> *have the same problem you have with the sonnet.*
> *Much too restrictive a form for minds like ours,*
> *wouldn't you say, old buddy? As I was telling*
> *Bob Frost just last week . . ."*

To help students make these sorts of connections with poetry, I have used a series of what I call "Hobnobbing Questions," questions that allow students to react to a poem as practicing writers of poetry. Answering these questions, they use the knowledge and experiences they have gained with their own poetic endeavors. I ask them to respond, in small groups or independently, to the assigned poems they are reading with questions like these:

- Select one or two of the author's most successful lines. Rearrange a few of the words. What makes the line work? What poetic elements did the author employ? How might a non-poet state the same thing?
- List the author's "star" words and strongest images. What makes them work? What process do you think the author went through to find them? Does the author also have some weak wordings?
- What do you suppose the author's "triggering experience" was? *Don't be afraid to guess!* Are there any clues within the poem about what caused the poet to write it?
- What associations did the author use that you relate to the most? Are there any associations you have with the subject of the poem that you would add?

Grappling with questions like these affords young writers the opportunity to take an insider's track and to see the world of poetry as true practitioners.

EVALUATIONS—HONING AND COACHING THE POETS

We have offered the student writer a wide and varied exposure to poetry; we have drawn from an array of activities available for stimulating creativity. We have experimented with word tinkering and offered writers' workshops. Given these and other poetry writing activities and strategies, there is still one element of the classroom writing process without which all other ingredients become essentially ineffectual: the student/teacher relationship. This is the communication the student feels she has with the teacher and the relationship the teacher has with the student and her writing. How a teacher responds to a student and her writing effort has a greater impact on that student and her eventual success with writing poetry than a footlocker full of writing strategies and methods.

We must always remember that for a student to find something he truly wants to say and then to say it well in a poem is a struggle requiring great persistence. To the student, the mountain may seem insurmountable, the rewards too vague. For students to take the risks involved and make themselves as vulnerable as they must in order to write good poetry, they must have sympathetic and knowledgeable mentors. We, as teacher-mentors, must sit alongside our students as both critical coaches and enthusiastic, sideline supporters. We need to be willing to become as vulnerable as the students and respond to and evaluate the poetry they write as honestly and sincerely as we can.

The greatest fear many teachers have in teaching poetry is how to judge writing endeavors and then how to respond appropriately to the students. Countless times teachers have told me that they love sharing poetry in their classes, reading and discussing many poems, but that they are terrified about how to judge, grade, respond to, talk about, or even just honestly react to the poems their students write. A few years ago, I was chairperson of the Young Authors' Conference for the Colorado Council of the International Reading Association. The conference held an annual writing contest for students throughout the state. Each year of my tenure, I had solicited teachers and friends to help me judge the nearly two thousand entries that were submitted. Each year, my "judges" were more than willing to participate, until the year that the contest category was poetry. "I'd really like to help again, Greg, but I am honestly afraid to judge a poem," or "I quite frankly don't know how to evaluate poetry," many of them confided.

Their fears and insecurities were well founded. Poetry *is* difficult to evaluate. There are no easy formulas or simple objective checklists on which to rely. A poem is in itself a single entity, a singular, creative voice. Each poem is different. There are, however, a few guidelines that I have found particularly useful.

- Enter into a partnership with the student.
- Always respond first to the student's intended meaning.
- Constantly refer to the student as a poet.
- Center your remarks around what makes good poetry in general and not necessarily on only what will make the immediate piece better.

I will talk about each of these separately.

Enter into a partnership with the student

A model I have used in my workshops (see Figure 6–10) suggests the direction of the relationship I have found to be most beneficial to the beginning student writer. (It also follows from my sense of what being a true teacher is.) I did not hold a textbook-Bible of right and wrong, of correct and incorrect, over their heads. I did not have them jump and grab for what the textbook said was right. Rather, I pulled up my chair next to the students and said, "Well, what are we going to learn today?" My comments and attitudes toward the students were as a senior learner, a partner in their poetry efforts: "I love this image right here, wish I'd thought of it" or "I've had the same problem with some of the poems I've written. How do you think we ought to solve it?"

Within a partnership, students move away from responses like "Is this right, Mr. D.?" to "What do you think about this line?" They know that they have the final say about their poems and that I am only a coach and sounding board. My suggestions are indirect, perhaps worded in this way: "You know, Michael, I was wondering, when I read your poem, about this part right here. I was kind of lost. I wanted to ask you what you were thinking." As with all healthy partnerships, each partner's comments and concerns are equally considered, and each respects the other's opinion. Each is ultimately interested in growth—in this case, the writing growth of the student.

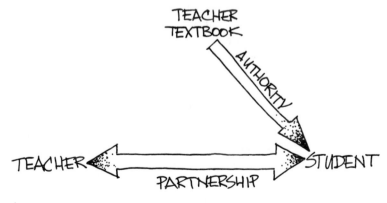

Figure 6–10

Always respond first to the student's intended meaning

My most important and immediate concern in reacting to a student's work is to respond somehow to its meaning—what it is the student is trying to say—no matter how awkward, sentimental, or uneven the attempt may be. "Gee, Judith, I didn't know you had so many problems with your older sister. Glad you wrote the poem about it. Sounds like she's a real pain." Or, "What a wonderful description of a sunrise, Jim—could I borrow your 'poet's glasses' when you're not using them?"

We can all remember some time in our schooling when we turned in a paper that was returned to us looking like a road map with a series of red lines and marks and not a comment as to what the paper was saying. Human beings, no matter what age, need to know that what they struggle to say is valued by others. This is not to suggest that after my initial response to the student's intended meaning I do not want to become the coach and take a closer look at the success of the piece.

Many times, my critical remarks about the success of the poem were camouflaged by the use of a continuum type of scoring (see Figure 6–11). This score sheet was modeled after a similar sheet found in *The Writing Process* textbook series published by Allyn and Bacon. I would circle the appropriate number to give the students a rating of their poetic accomplishments. These sheets were also used as self-evaluations or filled out by other students and brought to their small critics' circles as the basis of discussions of each other's poems.

Our personal judgment of a student's writing effort in a poem, simply stated, should stem first from what it is the student has attempted to say and then what success he has had in saying it. We should bear in mind that a student's language reflects his experiences in life and we should respect and judge his work in that light.

Constantly refer to the student as a poet

I remember when I submitted my first manuscript of poetry to a college literary magazine and was to meet the professor who was in charge of the magazine for a conference about the manuscript. Although I secretly fantasized that he would greet me as the American Dylan Thomas, I was, in reality, no fool. I knew my verse did not compare with what I read. I did not know how he would re-

POETRY PERFORMANCE SCORE CARD

1	2	3	4	5	6	7	8	9	10

Images

O.K., so where are they? You really mean you call that a poetic image? Come on!

Better . . . Play with your language more. Experiment with strange words in weird combinations. See what you come up with.

Wow . . . I love it! Vivid, startling, concrete, sensory images. This is poetic language at its best.

1	2	3	4	5	6	7	8	9	10

Word Choice

Hey! What's the matter? Don't you have any word imagination? You've got words in your head. Use them!

Getting better. Did you know that some poets look for months for the perfect word?

Now we're talking word choice! These are powerful. I couldn't have found any better words myself.

1	2	3	4	5	6	7	8	9	10

Feelings and Associations

Did a person or a machine write these? This sounds like a robot talking. No feeling. I want associations I can relate to.

Now I'm beginning to make the connections. Keep trying to have me feel what you felt, see what you saw, and be where you were.

Look out, publishing world— we've got a poet here. I was moved. Thank you.

1	2	3	4	5	6	7	8	9	10

Design

Did you ever hear of a line break? What do you think you're writing, a paragraph of prose?

That's better, but think DESIGN. How can I design my words and lines to go along with my meaning?

Hey, I like this! Your word placement drew me into the poem; it intrigued my eyes, as well as my ears.

Overall Score

Figure 6–11

spond. What he said had a great impact on me: "Greg, you think like a poet."

He did *not* say, "Greg, this is pure poetic genius. When can you meet with my publishers?" What he did say, in effect, was, "Greg, you're a member of the club; you think like a poet." He pointed out good aspects of my writing, as well as weaker areas. He then made suggestions for improvement. He did not suggest that when I mastered the use of meter or the sonnet form, then and only then would I become a poet. He said that I was already a participating member of the poetry club.

This sense of membership is crucial for students. Like me, they are not fools and know that, for the most part, their verse does not measure up to the quality of what they read, Yet, by constantly referring to them as poets, we tell them that they are members of the club. If we wait until we master something before we refer to ourselves as practitioners, we may never learn it. No child was ever required to hit a home run or snag a line drive *before* being allowed membership in the baseball club. We give that child his baseball glove and much encouragement and call him a baseball player. You play, therefore you're a member. The same should be true with the poetry "club." We give young writers strategies and encouragement and call them poets. You write, therefore you're a member.

In my writing workshops, I constantly acknowledged that my students were poets. "You're the poet," I would say. "You need to make the decision about how you want the piece to turn out." Throughout the year, we featured different students on the bulletin board as "Poet of the Week." When I read a student's writing aloud, I acknowledged the author by saying, " . . . by poet, Linda White." By convincing students early on that they are writers and poets, we prime the pump and hasten the point in time when they truly discover their writing selves.

Center your remarks around what makes good poetry in general, and not necessarily on only what will make the immediate piece better

When I was a small boy and in constant search of shortcuts, my mother would warn that if I walked across somebody's yard, my feet would burn footprints into the grass and I would be caught and in "big trouble." I am thirty-seven now and never once have my feet burned a print when I have strayed off the sidewalk somewhere. To this day, however, when I cross my neighbor's yard for a visit,

I habitually check as I go to see if I am leaving any smoldering evidence of my route. It is as if my mother's warning continues to echo in my head.

Similarly, certain warnings sound in my head as I write: "Show, don't tell," "Use concrete details," "Never end a sentence with a preposition." I have internalized writing advice from workshops I have attended or writing classes I have taken. Even though I do not always adhere to the advice I hear, the words still echo and are becoming a part of my writing behavior.

I like to think that the comments I make when talking with children about their poetry create the same effect in them. Lucy McCormick Calkins talks about the phenomenon of children internalizing the questions their teachers use in writing conferences, eventually asking these same questions of themselves when they write (Calkins 1986, 20). In the same way that statements echo in my head and affect my writing behavior, I want my ideas, such as "Use fresh, unexpected word choices," to become part of my students' "echo" when they write. I fervently hope that every time my students write a line, they are thinking that good poetry uses fresh, unexpected words.

The writing advice we give children during our talks with them about their poetry should be applicable to further writing endeavors. "I think the word 'gay' doesn't work" helps the child only with that one piece of work on that one day. Advice such as "Good poetry tries to use imagery that creates specific pictures in our heads" can later be applied to a new piece of work, another day, at another workshop. I use comments like "Remember what I've always told you about imagery?" "Can you find where your imagery is the most vivid and where it is too vague?" In this way, I hope to have children apply generalized words of advice to their next poem.

So, what specific comments do I want echoing in my students' heads long after I have closed my workshop doors for the last time? Well, I hope that "Mr. D.'s three C's for writing poetry" will eternally haunt them. Enhancing and expanding from there, I would advise:

- Always use fresh, unexpected word choices.
- Avoid syrupy language.
- Find startling images that your reader's mind will react to.
- Chisel away unnecessary words.
- Use vivid, concrete, sensory details.
- Offer powerful and meaningful associations to your reader.

- Try to discover the music of each line.
- HONOR YOUR THOUGHTS WITH YOUR BEST EFFORT.

In the long run, we can only do our best at coaching and evaluating the poetic endeavors of our students. We can't be expected
to be the masters of all subjects—only conscious learners. Our
success as teachers of poetry will have less to do with what we
know and more to do with who we are. For, at the moment, we
are talking with a child about his writing—we are one person in
human contact with another, one learner with another. Students
react to us and to the fact that we are willing to learn alongside
them. I truly believe that my success as a reading teacher had little
to do with what I believe to be fine undergraduate training. It was
due, instead, to the fact that I was a reader, a lover of books, and
consequently, an ongoing learner about reading. The same is true
of my work with children and their poetry. Whatever degree of
success I had came from the fact that I was a reader and writer of
poetry and a fellow learner. No methods course or teaching technique can substitute for a partnership.

FINDING ONE'S OWN WORDS

As I conclude this chapter on the writing of poetry, it may surprise
the reader to know that I, the ultimate poetry enthusiast, did not
necessarily want all my students to become poets. Although I truly
believe that this beautiful (however fragile and, at times, troubled)
planet of ours could use many more fine poets, I did not try to make
poets out of every one of my students. There's no doubt that we all
benefit from the compassion poetry often brings out in us. And
believing as I do that all of us could potentially live more fully as
members of the human race with the benefit of the perceptions and
inspirations poets can capture in their words, nonetheless I do not
believe our language arts goals should include trying to mold our
students into poets.

Our planet equally needs doctors and teachers, engineers and
ministers, housewives/househusbands, and painters, comedians,
and baseball players. These may or may not be occupations that
also include the writing of poetry. The world needs and asks
only that we all develop our own talents in our own ways, living out our dreams and aspirations in occupations and pastimes
that bring the most meaning and fulfillment to our own individual lives.

Furthermore, I honestly do not believe I can teach a single soul to write poetry. If an individual is to write poetry seriously, that person will literally teach himself or herself. I can at best be only an early mentor. And by the same token, I doubt if I could actually prevent someone from becoming a poet. Every poet I know contends that he or she would have written poetry with or without a formal education, with or without the possibility of publishing books, with or without any monetary rewards, even without recognition. People write poetry because it is in their blood and because it makes them feel more fully alive and conscious of the very act of living.

Why, then, with the potential of so little tangible reward and even less chance of actually teaching the art to students, do I bother to teach the writing of poetry? Why do we need to struggle with the numerous wordsmithing exercises and the tedious management of writing workshops and student writing conferences during an already overloaded school day? Would our teaching time, not to mention our nerves, be better spent concentrating on more practical, more job-related skills?

No, I do not believe so.

Our poetry lessons, our writing workshops—all the activities we include in our language arts curriculum—teach one thing: that language can be manipulated by humans. We are, by our very evolution, linguistic beasts, and with that nature we can create more pleasing and successful and moving ways to use words. Words therefore become one of the most powerful inventions of humankind. Our language arts teach that we need not be subservient to or limited by the confines of our language and its words. Language is *our* willing and ready servant.

Our poetry instruction fits itself into the language arts "tool chest," in which students can find the means for discovering their own words. They can find words with which they can articulate who they are and what is important and meaningful to them, words they can use to attain a desired effect on others around them. Whether our students find the words to write beautiful poetry that stirs the hearts and minds of generations of peoples or simply find the right words to profess their love or propose marriage, the composition process is the same. And we have given them the tools. Whether they find the words and the way to express them that sway the decision of a jury, or simply quiet, heartfelt words that express condolences on a card to a friend, the learning is of equal value. They have used language to serve them, and we, as teachers, have given the students the right and necessary means.

Products of the language tool chest are all around us.

It was his ability to use the tools of language and pound out the right words and the right expressions that allowed the young President John F. Kennedy to ignite the imagination of the country as well as the entire free world with the words,

> Ask not what your country can do for you—
> ask what you can do for your country.

And it was with the same tools that a black minister from Atlanta, Georgia, found his words:

> I have a dream . . . Free at last!
> Free at last! Thank God Almighty,
> we are free at last!

Dr. Martin Luther King stood up and stirred the conscience of a confused and embattled country.

It was through the same wordsmithing skills that a Paul McCartney-John Lennon and a Bob Dylan impassioned an entire generation of young people with the lyrics of their songs.

The skills students acquire in our poetry-writing workshops are meant to serve them long after the cute, penciled poems have faded from the school paper, long after the glued limericks have fallen out of the hand-bound books, long after the extra school literary magazines have been moved for the last time from the school basement. To the extent that we succeed in our teaching, these skills will last the course of a lifetime of speaking, thinking, writing, and reading.

EPILOGUE
"Becoming Friendly"

Not long ago I was involved in a series of poetry workshops and performances in rural Missouri through a grant from the Missouri Arts and Humanities Council. On one of the mornings I was performing for a group of youngsters in an old one-room schoolhouse nearly hidden from sight among full sections of farmland ready for harvest. Toward the end of the session, a woman came in quietly and stood in the back of the room where I was speaking. When I was finished, the woman came up and asked, "You the man doing the poetry?" I explained that I was, and she reached out a faded, handwritten page of school paper. I could see immediately that it had been folded for many years. "Would you read this?"

I read the page. It was a poem, a touching but awkward attempt at a poetic rendering of a sad experience of the woman. The incident had occurred when she was eighteen (I guessed she was in her late thirties now). She and a group of her teenage girlfriends had been in a serious automobile accident somewhere along those narrow farm roads. The poem had been written a few years later in memory of two of the girls who had died in that accident.

She and I talked for only a moment about the poem. She had come neither for advice nor with the hope that I could get the poem published. I truly believe she had come simply to share her poem with me, someone she assumed understood this thing called "poetry." In searching for something to say, I asked her if she had ever shown the poem to anyone else. She shyly shook her head. After a moment she thanked me and turned toward the door, saying she must get back to her farm. "Chores are never done on the farm, you know."

I walked outside with the woman, saying good-bye and thanking her for coming, but I noticed that there was no car in front of the school. "How are you getting home?" I asked.

"I'm walking," she stated.

"Oh, is your farm close?" I asked.

"Over there." She pointed to a silo in the distance.

In surprise I estimated that the silo was a good ten miles away. Then it struck me. This woman had walked ten miles to share a personal poem with someone she had never met. It saddened me to think how long she had waited before she felt she could share her story and the words she had chosen to tell about her experience. As I watched her disappear down the road, I silently hoped that no child would ever have to wait so long or walk so far simply to share his or her work with a stranger.

What had motivated this woman so far from the halls of academia, normally associated with art forms such as poetry, to draft out this poem? Her life on the farm stood to gain nothing of substance. In fact, other than myself, I'm not sure anyone else would ever see the poem. What purpose did it serve?

Lucy McCormick Calkins, in her excellent book *The Art of Teaching Writing*, suggests that humans have a deep need to write, to "represent their experience through writing."

> We need to make our truths beautiful. With crude pictographs, cave men inscribed their stories onto stony cave walls. With magic markers, pens, lipstick, and pencils, little children leave their marks on bathroom walls, on the backs of old envelopes, on their big sister's homework. In slow, wobbly letters, the old and the sick in our nursing homes and hospitals put their lives into print. There is no plot line in the bewildering complexity of our lives but that which we make and find for ourselves. By

articulating experience, we reclaim it for ourselves. Writing allows us to turn the chaos into something beautiful, to frame selected moments in our lives, to uncover and to celebrate the organizing patterns of our existence. (Calkins 1986, 3)

This quiet and unassuming woman in Missouri had acted out of that need. She'd attempted to capture in words a tragic but significant moment of her life. She could easily have confined her grief to a back corner of her heart or maybe only told the story as a recollection to her family around the kitchen table or to her friends at the café in town. Instead, she chose to use that unique gift that separated her from other life forms—her innate linguistic capacity, her ability to use words and to find comfort through the expression of those words. Furthermore, she had attempted, to the degree of her own capability, to make a memorable arrangement of those words—one that would last. She was not all that different from ancient kings who employed troubadours to tell of their deeds, using ballads to immortalize them and their lives and feats. Somehow this woman instinctively knew that by choosing to use poetry she might give life back to her friends—at least in her words.

By articulating her experience as best she could, this woman had taken a step toward joining and becoming a part of the literate world—a world predicated on a proficiency with language. She had, in a sense, "become friendly" with the community of words and assumed her right to stand shoulder to shoulder with all who use and have used written language.

Having children become friendly with the community of words and lay claim to their linguistic heritage is the dream of all inspired teachers—and, we hope, not just with poetry, but with story and song, essay and narrative, diary and letter, and all forms of language usage. Having our students develop the capacity for expressing complex and diverse dimensions of thought should be the goal of all education. We, as teachers, are already members-at-large of the language community and through our instruction and modeling we invite our students into full membership also. But children don't make broad leaps head first into the world of literacy. They begin tentatively, with small steps.

I'll always remember the thank-you note given to me by a ruffled-haired first grader after I visited his class.

Mr. Poemteller,
Thank you for coming.
I injond your

> coming. I'm writing
> 4 poems. 2 poems
> that don't rime
> and 2 that dose rime.

Think of it: a small step of only four simple poems to begin a lifelong association with poetry—two that "don't rime" and two that "dose rime." I sincerely hope he's found and continues to find *his* rhymes.

As babies need supportive adult hands holding and balancing them while they take their first steps, so our students need support as they make their way into the literate world. In this regard Shirley Brice Heath takes a most powerful educational stance in her book *Ways with Words* when she suggests that the single most important condition for literary-learning is the presence of mentors who are joyfully literate persons.

So who are these "joyfully literate mentors"? They come in all shapes. I've heard of and met many:

- A principal in Albuquerque, New Mexico, who, when the children gather around him on the playgrounds, recites poetry. I've watched them beg for their favorite piece.
- A mother who, when she walks her six-year-old in the park, tries to discover how many words and phrases the two of them can think up to describe the sky, the trees, the lake, and the people.
- A janitor-poet who, when he cleans the blackboards in the classrooms of a major university, leaves wonderful poems on them for the morning classes.
- Someone in a Montana state park who leaves poems written on stones along the trail to delight the eyes and ears of the hikers.
- A school librarian in a small Colorado town who writes poems on large billboards that she hangs around her neck. She walks in and out of classrooms unannounced, sharing a quick poem or two.
- A tour bus driver in California who recites long narrative poems to his passengers. At the end of each trip, he is reported to say, "Well, I don't know how much you got out of the tour, but I hope you enjoyed the poetry."

My list could go on. I hope that I am mentor to the participants in my workshops and the readers of this book. Each of us has the potential for being that "joyfully literate mentor" for the children with whom we are in association. Through our own joy we can set the stage for children to evolve into readers of poetry.

Poetry, by all measures, is not as popular today as it was in the past. We seem to have passed through the era when people read poetry regularly. Our brave new world has many more things competing for our attention than was the case in our grandparents' time. But poetry is as *important* as it always was. It served the woman from Missouri in the same way it has served and will continue to serve all of humanity. For poetry will always draw on the human need of all people to hold on to bits of their lives, fragments of the human experience, and moments of their cultural past. In the end, poetry makes our lives and our language more beautiful.

William W. Holland, in an article entitled "The Unseen Worth" written for *The Christian Science Monitor*, recalls a dream he had several months after taking his first poetry class as an adult. In the dream his teacher, Larry Roab, asked, "Why is poetry like the gold in Fort Knox?" Holland, in a moment of rare clarity, made the final connection between all that he had learned in the class. Suddenly everything came together—the poems, the discussion, the bits and pieces of fragmented understandings. He rose to his feet and bravely answered:

Without the gold in Fort Knox, our currency would lose its value. Poetry is like the gold in Fort Knox, because even though not many ever see it, the value of the language depends on it. (Holland 1982, 20)

It is my fondest dream that the children in your classes *do* get to visit "Fort Knox"—and in the process get to keep some of that gold to call their own.

LETTER TO READERS

.

Readers,

The French poet Paul Valéry once said that a poem is never finished, only abandoned. So, too, this book. When one attempts the laborious task of talking-with-words-on-paper about a topic he knows and loves, there is a persistent, nagging feeling of not having said it all, an unsettling sense of incompleteness.

There will always be another point I wanted to make in this book, another illustration I would have loved to share, one last example to tie it all together, or one more book to which I wanted to refer. If, however, I have done my writing job well, then that may legitimately become the responsibility of you, the book's readers. You need to make the points I have failed to make, discover the connections I have overlooked, and seek on your own the best poems and teaching strategies to use in your classrooms from the ideas I have only begun to uncover. You have the opportunity to explore more deeply under the rocks I have stumbled on and overturned. Quite honestly, I believe that to be the joy of teaching. And, it is certainly what keeps us young.

So, as I often tell my university students on the last day of class, "There's much more I have to say, but for now I believe I've said enough."

RESOURCES

"Seeds"—Poetry Activities

A "Buddhist teaching story" entitled "A Single Grain of Rice," goes, much too briefly, like this:

> A king calls his four daughters together and explains that he is going away and that they are to rule the kingdom in his absence. Before he leaves, he gives each of them a single grain of rice and tells them to "do the best you can" with the rice and to be prepared to show him their grains of rice if he should return. Consequently, each daughter does something different with the rice, trying to comply with the father's order. Many years later, the king returns, quite old by this time, and asks to see the rice. Each daughter gives her father a grain of rice, except for the last, who no longer has the original grain. She has planted it and watched it multiply into many fine rice fields. The fourth daughter, of course, has done the very best and receives the king's crown.

I hope this final section of the book gives you not one, but many poetry "seeds" that you can plant in your classroom and, like the fourth daughter, that you discover that each of them grows and blossoms into many more poetry activities for you to use.

I. POEMS WITH DIFFERING RHYME SCHEMES

- "Twickham Tweer" by Jack Prelutsky
- "Rhyme" by Elizabeth Coatsworth
- "A Bug Sat in a Silver Flower" by Karla Kuskin

- "Mother's Nerves" by X. J. Kennedy
- "Whispers" by Myra Cohn Livingston
- "Alone in the Garage" by Gregory Harrison
- "If I Were King" by A. A. Milne
- "Homework" by Russell Hoban
- "The Runaway" by Bobbi Katz
- "Lines and Squares" by A. A. Milne

Have youngsters interweave the different rhyme schemes with their crayons and colored pencils to notice the many different ways poets choose to use the "word performance" of rhyme. They may want to start "rhyming word banks" in their Poetry Notebooks:

bean
lean
jean
seem
green

. . . in hopes, of course, of stumbling on those "rare rhymes" that will delight the ears of their readers.

II. BOOKS WITH DISTINCTIVE LANGUAGE PATTERNS

- *I Can't Said the Ant* by Polly Cameron
- *If All the Seas Were One Sea* by Janina Domanska
- *If I Were a Cricket* by Kazue Mizumura
- *Good Night, Mr. Beetle* by Leland B. Jacobs
- *Bears* by Ruth Krauss
- *Brown Bear, Brown Bear, What Do You See?* by Bill Martin Jr
- *I Paint Joy of a Flower* by Bill Martin Jr
- *Whistle, Mary, Whistle* by Bill Martin Jr
- *If It Weren't for You* by Charlotte Zolotow
- *Someday* by Charlotte Zolotow
- *Gentle, Gentle Thursday* by Gene D. Shepard and Bill Martin Jr
- *A Maker of Boxes* by H. R. Wright
- *What Is That Sound!* by Mary O'Neill
- *Hailstones and Halibut Bones* by Mary O'Neill

Allow the youngsters to begin their first forays into writing their own poems with the help of the "artist's invisible hand." Cloth-bound books with illustrations made by the kids make the writing memorable.

III. CONCRETE POEMS TO "EYE" FOR THE APPRECIATION OF WORD PLACEMENT

- "Spring Is" by Bobby Katz
- "Two in Bed" by A. B. Ross
- "Seal" by William Jay Smith
- "Easy Diver" by Robert Froman

Viewing concrete poems not only sensitizes the eye to the potential of word placement but also gives young readers and writers the impression that poems can do more on the page than simply "mean." Have your classes take their own poems and discover interesting ways to create designs with their words.

IV. POEMS THAT HAVE CREATIVE MOVEMENT POSSIBILITIES

- "Bubble Gum" by Nina Payne
- "Winter Clothes" by Karla Kuskin
- "From: A Christmas Package" by David McCord
- "Hug o'War" by Shel Silverstein
- "Wiggly Giggles" by Stacy Jo Crossen and Natalie Anne Covell
- "The Land of Counterpane" by Robert Louis Stevenson
- "The Little Turtle" by Vachel Lindsay

By themselves, with a friend, or in a group, children ache to move with poetry. Designate an out-of-the-way area of the room where they can dance, move, and clap with the poems.

V. POEMS THAT BLEND WELL FOR CHORAL READINGS

- "Spring Morning" by A. A. Milne
- "If I Were King" by A. A. Milne

- "On Mother's Day" by Aileen Fisher
- "The Three Singing Birds" by James Reeves
- "Three Little Kittens" traditional
- "The Romp" by Nancy Byrd Turner

Choral readings may be one of the easiest access routes leading children into the realm of the sound of poetry. They are always a big hit as an evening program for parents. Have the youngsters break the poems into sections, assign narrators and solo parts, differentiate between characters, and then enjoy the poem together.

VI. POEMS THAT BEG TO BE DRAMATIZED

- "The Cremation of Sam McGee" by Robert Service
- "Snowman" by Shel Silverstein
- "At the Garden Gate" by David McCord
- "The Three Little Kittens" by Eliza Lee Follen
- "Sometimes I Feel This Way" by John Ciardi
- "Mummy Slept Late and Daddy Fixed Breakfast" by John Ciardi
- "The Old Wife and the Ghost" by James Reeves
- "Colonel Fazackerley" by Charles Causley

The many exciting ways youngsters come up with to dramatize a poem never cease to amaze me. Give them time and room to make a few of these poems their own—Shakespeare style!

VII. POEMS WITH CLEAR EXAMPLES OF FIGURATIVE LANGUAGE

- "April Rain Song" by Langston Hughes
- "Autumn" by Emily Dickinson
- "Spring" by Karla Kuskin
- "Winter Poem" by Nikki Giovanni
- "rain or hail" by e e cummings
- "The New Year" by Dinah Maria Mulock Craik
- "On a Snowy Day" by Dorothy Aldis
- "Back Yard Swing" by Myra Cohn Livingston

Help your students walk comfortably in the "metaphoric dimension" of poetry by noticing the simple metaphors and similes and examples of personification within poems like these. Have them record the metaphor language in their Poetry Notebooks.

VIII. POEMS WITH NATURAL LEAD-INS TO DISCUSSIONS AND WRITING TOPICS

- "The World Is Not a Pleasant Place to Be" by Nikki Giovanni
  Is the world a hard place to be?
  Do we need someone to make our lives complete?
  Why is it important to have a partner?
- "Leavetaking" by Eve Merriam
  What are your feelings at the end of a vacation?
- "History" by Myra Cohn Livingston
  What have you dreamed about during history?
- "Rules" by Karla Kuskin
  What are some rules you think of as ridiculous?
  Create a set of "Ridiculous Rules" that people should live by.
- "Two People" by Eve Merriam
  How are your parents different from each other?
  How are you different from one of your friends?
  Can differences make stronger ties between people?
- "In the Motel" by X. J. Kennedy
  Do you remember a driving trip with your family?
  What was it like in the back seat?
  What did you do to pass the time?
  Make up a new travel game to play in order to pass the time.
- "True Story" by Shel Silverstein
  Write your own tall tale.
  Rewrite in poetic language a tall tale you know.
- "A Dream About the Man in the Moon" by John Ciardi
  Write one of your own strange dreams as a poem.
- "Lines and Squares" by A. A. Milne
  What kinds of superstitions do you have or can you remember having?
- "Up in the attic there's a great big trunk
     Full of jangling, jellified Halloween junk . . . "
  (Untitled, from *Blackberry Ink* by Eve Merriam)
  Find a trunk in your own imagination.
  Write rhyming couplets about what you find inside.

- "The Runaway" by Bobbi Katz
  Write about a time you ran away.
  What was it like?
  How did you feel?
- "Jack and the Beanstalk" by Roald Dahl
  Retell one of your favorite fairy tales as a poem.

IX. POEMS THAT WAIT TO BE ARTISTICALLY EXPRESSED

You can bring poetry and art experiences together in many wonderful ways. Below is a "starter's kit."

ART

"Roads" by Rachel Field

Objective: To teach construction and perception skills through the creation of a model town. This is to be a group project.

Materials: Colored construction paper, tape, glue, scissors, butcher paper covering a table.

Procedure: After reading the poem a few times, brainstorm ideas the students have about interesting places to which a road might lead. List these on the board. Have a few students draw a road on the butcher paper. Each student can create his or her own imaginative place to be set up along the community road. Before setting students loose with this, it would be wise to review three-dimensional building skills (constructing a cylinder, a cube, a box, a cone; the use of tabs for older students). Be sure to encourage the addition of lots of details like doors, windows, shutters, tiles, shingles, and environmental stuff like trees, flowers, paths, etc.

Suggestions: To encourage the imaginations of the students, it would be good to display photographs or reproductions of lots of different kinds of housing and environments around the room.

ART

"The Balloon" by Karla Kuskin

Objective: To create a print inspired by the impressions formed by the poem.

Materials: Tempera paint, brushes, colored construction paper, chalk, found objects to print with such as buttons, wooden spools, bottlecaps, mailing tubes, corks (or any round objects).

Procedure: This poem presents the perfect inspiration for a successful printmaking experience. Students choose a piece of construction paper, use a brush to apply tempera paint to the found objects, and press the object on the paper to obtain a print. Repeating shapes leads to unity in the composition. Background can be put in with chalk after the print has dried. Encourage students to illustrate images from the poem in their backgrounds.

ART

"Very Early" by Karla Kuskin

Objective: To create a crayon engraving of images suggested by the poem. Students will be expected to use overlapping to present a unified image.

Materials: Wax crayons, oak-tag board, sharp utensil such as a knife or dental tool.

Procedure: Using light-colored crayons, cover the entire surface of the oak-tag board (any size) with a heavy application of color. Follow this with a coat of black crayon. Students should do preliminary drawings on paper the size of the board. When satisfied with an image, scratch the design through the black crayon with the sharp tool.

Suggestions: The technique of crayon engraving itself is prompted by the images in the poem. As the students scratch away the black crayon and uncover the light, bright colors, they can almost feel that awakening suggested in the poem. Each student should have a copy of the poem before the preliminary drawing stage. Encourage the use of images made clear in the poem, as well as more personal ideas. The use of overlapping can be reviewed (or introduced) as a way to help several images become a unified whole.

ART

"Our House" by Dorothy Brown Thompson

Objective: To create a drawing with line variation and interest.

Materials: White drawing paper and choice of pencil, crayon, pen, or marker.

Procedure: As a homework assignment, have your students choose a favorite place in their home. Find a quiet time to sit and draw that area using any one of the materials suggested. Encourage them to include lots of objects and details in the drawing. Attention should be drawn to the quality of lines used, rather than color. Vary lines with pressure, width, or emphasis. When giving this assignment, it would be helpful to demonstrate some lines, including delicate, bold, rhythmic, and dynamic lines. Have the students demonstrate some lines that they create.

ART

"October Magic" by Myra Cohn Livingston

Objective: To create a unified mural portraying many students' ideas of Halloween.

Materials: Butcher paper, chalk, tempera paint.

Procedure: Find a space low enough for your students to work on and cover it with butcher paper. Put a tarp on the floor. Students should lay out ideas on drawing paper after reading and discussing the poem. When they are satisfied with their portrayal of Halloween ideas, small groups of students may begin drawing on the mural with chalk. The teacher may see opportunities to encourage overlapping of shapes, grouping objects or figures for unity, and using a variety in sizes and shapes and in the breakup of space in both foreground and background. The placement of objects is important in a mural (use larger figures at the bottom, smaller ones higher up to create the illusion of space). When the class is satisfied with the composition, a few students may be chosen to paint all the chalk lines with black tempera. Students may then add color with tempera or chalk. Background colors will help unify the composition of the mural.

ART

"The Toaster" by William Jay Smith

Objective: To introduce surrealism and have the student create a surrealistic painting.

Materials: Reproductions of work by Salvador Dali, watercolor paper, pencil, watercolors.

Procedure: Read the poem and brainstorm student ideas about other everyday objects and the dreamlike things that they could do. Introduce students to the Surrealist art movement in which artists tried to portray dreams directly from the unconscious mind onto the canvas. Challenge students to choose one image to portray in a painting. Draw in pencil on the watercolor paper; then paint with watercolors.

Suggestions: Encourage drawing in large scale so important details can be included.

ART

"Have You Watched the Fairies?" by Rose Fyleman

Objective: To study texture through the creation of a collage.

Materials: Colored construction paper, glue, scissors, ink pens, variety of collage materials such as lace, ribbon, tissue paper, aluminum foil, netting, pipe cleaners, plastic wrap.

Procedure: Each student may choose a color of construction paper. Collage materials should be in a central location for easy access by students. After reading and discussing the poem, lead a brainstorming session on all the types of fairies thought of by your students. List these on the board. Students may choose one or several types of fairies and create their wings using the collage materials. They may want to label each wing with the names of the fairies.

Suggestions: When discussing each student's work, point out the variety of textures used.

ART

"The Mirror" by A. A. Milne

Objective: To use repetition to create unity in a collage.

Materials: Colored construction paper, scissors, glue, watercolors, 10" × 24" white paper.

Procedure: The students choose five or six 4" × 8" sheets of colored construction paper (may be the same or different colors). Fold each in half to form a 4" × 4" square and cut a different shape out of each, leaving the fold intact. These can be animal shapes, geometric shapes, free shapes, etc. Glue these on the white paper, lining up the fold lines. Use watercolors to add to the background, painting in added reflections if the students wish. Details may be added to the shapes with cut pieces of paper or with crayons.

Suggestions: Point out the use of repetition inherent in the collages through the reflections. Suggest the unifying aspect of that repetition.

X. POETRY ACTIVITY SHEETS

Activity sheets that can be done independently or in pairs are excellent ways for children to extend their knowledge of poetry. Here are a few I used with my youngsters. Notice how I helped them see with the poet's eyes in this first one.

IMAGININ' WITH YOUR OWN EYES ... READ THE ARTICLE • CLOSE YOUR EYES. SEE THE "LITTLE LAME BALLOONMAN" IN YOUR HEAD • WRITE AS MANY DESCRIPTIVE WORDS ABOUT HIM AS YOU CAN.

IMAGININ' WITH THE POET'S EYES ... READ THE POEM • CLOSE YOUR EYES. SEE THE "LITTLE LAME BALLOONMAN" AS THE POET DESCRIBED HIM • COPY THE WORDS THE POET USED IN HIS DESCRIPTION.

Children Report Seeing Balloonman Again

Children living in town have reported seeing the man they call the "little lame balloonman" again this spring. "We know when he's here by his whistle," they say. Although the reports have been unconfirmed, it appears that a lame man with balloons appears out of nowhere in our town every spring. He reportedly never says much — just whistles and kids run to him. No one knows where he comes from or where he goes in the winter.

Title _____

Author _____

From _____

Here I allow them to make their own predictions prior to reading.

WONDERIN'
1. READ THE ARTICLE. WRITE AS MANY QUESTIONS AS POP INTO YOUR HEAD. COMPARE YOUR QUESTIONS WITH A FRIEND'S QUESTIONS.

PREDICTIN'
2. ANSWER YOUR QUESTIONS. YOU MAY END UP ONLY GUESSING. COMPARE YOUR ANSWERS WITH YOUR FRIEND'S ANSWERS.

Girl Claims To Have Met "Green Fiddler"

A young girl in a neighboring village has reported that while she was walking in the nearby hills she ran into a "little green man" who asked her for four strands of golden hair. "He then threaded my hair into his fiddle and played music like I've never imagined before," she stated. Doctors are now concerned that the girl acts as if she has some special secret deep in her heart and seems to have lost all interest in what others think of her.

Title _____

Author _____

From _____

3. NOW, READ THE POEM AND COMPARE BOTH YOUR ANSWERS WITH THE ONES YOU FOUND IN THE POEM.

And here I have them activate what they already know about the American pioneers before coming to know Stephen Vincent Benét's William Sycamore:

COMIN' TO KNOW SOMEONE

Book Review

The Ballad of William Sycamore
by Stephen Vincent Benét
(Farrar & Rinehart, Inc., New York)
Reviewed by Gregory Denman

1. LIST AS MANY WORDS AS YOU THINK OF WHEN YOU ENVISION THE AMERICAN PIONEER:

_____
_____
_____
_____
_____
_____
_____

In his new ballad, Stephen Vincent Benét utilizes characteristically impeccable adherence to detail in tracing the life of authentic American pioneer, William Sycamore.

Benét writes brilliantly of Sycamore's austere beginnings in rural Kentucky. Sycamore's father was a mountaineer, and his mother gave birth to William while kneeling beside a mountain stream. Raised in a log cabin, the boy vividly recalls occasional visits from other mountain people who would dance until "the dried herbs rattled above the door," while Will's father called the numbers.

Sycamore joined the American surge west. Following the trail of western wagons, he and his young wife reared two boys along the way. The ballad includes the tragic loss of Sycamore's two sons; the elder son died at the Alamo, and his younger brother gave his life in the Battle of Little Big Horn.

Benét's ballad is most moving as he recounts Sycamore's struggle later in life as civilization catches up with him. He is devastated as the wide open west is fenced off and towns spring up where once there had been open prairies. In despair, Sycamore saddles an unbroken colt and rides off not knowing where to go. He is eventually killed by the colt.

The last scene, in which William Sycamore is dying, is one of the most moving passages found in American literature. In it, the reader senses the end of the pioneer era, but not the end of this man's indomitable spirit. "The Ballad of William Sycamore" should be required reading for all those interested in the American experience.

2. DISCOVER FIVE FACTS ABOUT THE LIFE OF WILLIAM SYCAMORE FROM THE ARTICLE.

① _____
② _____
③ _____
④ _____
⑤ _____

3. FROM YOUR READING OF THE POEM, HOW MANY OF THE IDEAS BEHIND YOUR DESCRIPTIVE WORDS WERE IN THE POEM? HOW MANY FACTS ABOUT WILLIAM SYCAMORE'S LIFE WERE ALSO IN THE POEM?

Here's an excellent activity to tie a poem in with the study of grammar.

READ "JABBERWOCKY" AND FILL IN THE LIST. PLEASE DO THIS ON YOUR OWN PAPER.

JABBERWOCKY: Using Your Word Sense!

nouns	verbs	adjectives	adverbs	prepositional phrases

Children always write unusual newspaper articles about poems.

ON YOUR OWN

NOTICE HOW I TOOK THE POEM AND WROTE A NEWSPAPER ARTICLE ABOUT IT • TRY WRITING YOUR OWN NEWSPAPER ARTICLE FROM ANOTHER POEM • . . . . . . SHARE IT WITH A FRIEND •

Whose woods these are I think I know.
His house is in the village though;
He will not see me stopping here
To watch his woods fill up with snow.

My little horse must think it queer
To stop without a farmhouse near
Between the woods and frozen lake
The darkest evening of the year.

He gives his harness bells a shake
To ask if there is some mistake.
The only other sound's the sweep
Of easy wind and downy flake.

The woods are lovely, dark, and deep.
But I have promises to keep,
And miles to go before I sleep,
And miles to go before I sleep.

Stranger Arrives

Out of the darkest night of this bitter winter a stranger arrived early this morning. Police report that he must have become delirious from being out in the snow all night because he just repeated the same words – "and miles to go before I sleep."

Title _____

Author _____

From _____

Finally, why not let your class adopt-a-poet? You'll find a list of good poets in this book.

ADOPT - A - POET

ADOPT-A-POET   NAME _____

POET

BORN

BACKGROUND

WHAT PEOPLE HAVE SAID ABOUT MY POET

REASON FOR ADOPTION

Children's Poets

Poets for younger children

Dorothy Aldis
Gwendolyn Brooks
Margaret Wise Brown
Lewis Carroll
John Ciardi
Beatrice Schenk de Regniers
Emily Dickinson
Eleanor Farjeon
Eugene Field
Aileen Fisher
Kathleen Fisher
Nikki Giovanni
Eloise Greenfield
Margaret Hillert
Lee Bennett Hopkins

Patricia Hubbell
Leland B. Jacobs
X. J. Kennedy
Karla Kuskin
Nancy Larrick
Dennis Lee
Myra Cohn Livingston
David McCord
Bill Martin Jr
Eve Merriam
A. A. Milne
Lilian Moore
Maurice Sendak
Charlotte Zolotow

Poets for middle-grade youngsters

Byrd Baylor
Harry Behn
Stephen Vincent Benét
John Ciardi
e e cummings
Walter de la Mare
Eleanor Farjeon
Rachel Field
Frances Frost
Robert Frost
Langston Hughes
Ted Hughes
Edna St. Vincent Millay

Evaline Ness
Mary O'Neill
Jack Prelutsky
Laura E. Richards
James Whitcomb Riley
Theodore Roethke
Carl Sandburg
Lew Sarret
Shel Silverstein
Robert Louis Stevenson
James Tripplet
Judith Viorst

Poetry Selections

Adoff, Arnold, ed. *City in All Directions*. Macmillan.

————. *Eats: Poems*. Lothrop.

Adshead, Gladys L. *An Inheritance of Poetry*. Houghton Mifflin.

Aiken, Joan. *The Song Spinners*. Viking.

Arbuthnot, May Hill. *Time for Poetry*. Scott, Foresman.

Atwood, Ann. *Haiku-Vision*. Scribner's.

Behn, Harry. *The Golden Hive*. Harcourt Brace.

————. *The Little Hill*. Harcourt Brace.

————. *The Wizard in the Well*. Harcourt Brace.

Benét, Stephen Vincent. *The Ballad of William Sycamore*. Little, Brown.

Blishen, Edward. *Oxford Book of Poetry for Children*. Oxford.

Bontemps, Arna. *Hold Fast to Dreams*. Follett.

Brewton, Sara; John Brewton; and John Brewton Blackburn, eds. *Of Quarks, Quasars, and Other Quirks: Quizzical Poems for the Super Sonic Age*. Crowell.

Brown, Margaret Wise. *Nibble Nibble*. Addison-Wesley.

Ciardi, John. *Fast and Slow*. Houghton Mifflin.

————. *The Man Who Sang the Sillies*. Lippincott.

————. *The Reason for the Pelican*. Lippincott.

————. *Someone Could Win a Polar Bear*. Lippincott.

————. *You Know Who*. Lippincott.

————. *You Read to Me, I'll Read to You*. Lippincott.

Cole, William. *The Birds and the Beasts Were There*. Collins & World.

————. *Humorous Poetry for Children*. World (Canada).

————. *Poem Stew*. Harper & Row.

————. *Poems for Seasons and Celebrations*. Collins & World.

————. *Poems of Magic and Spells*. Collins & World.

————. *A Poet's Tale: A New Book of Story Poems*. World (Canada).

————. *Story Poems: Old and New*. Collins & World.

Cummings, E. E. *Hist Whist and Other Poems for Children*. Liveright.

de la Mare, Walter. *Peacock Pie*. Faber.

de Paola, Tomie. *Tomie de Paola's Mother Goose*. Putnam.

de Regniers, Beatrice Schenk. *Poems Children Will Sit Still For: A Selection for the Primary Grades*. Citation Press.

Dickinson, Emily. *Poems for Youth*. Little Brown.

Dunning, Stephen. *Reflections on a Gift of Watermelon Pickle and Other Modern Verse*. Scholastic.

Farber, Norma. *Never Say Ugh! to a Bug*. Morrow.

Ferris, Helen. *Favorite Poems: Old and New*. Doubleday.

Fisher, Aileen. *Out in the Dark and Daylight*. Harper & Row.

Felleman, Hazel. *Poems That Live Forever*. Doubleday.

Frost, Robert. *Stopping by Woods on a Snowy Evening*. Dutton.

————. *A Swinger of Birches*. Stemmer House.

————. *You Come Too*. Holt, Rinehart & Winston.

Godden, Rumer. *Prayers from the Ark: The Creatures' Choir*. Penguin.

Hopkins, Lee Bennett. *By Myself*. Crowell.

————. *Crickets, Bullfrogs, and Whispers*. Harcourt Brace Jovanovich.

————. *A Dog's Life*. Harcourt Brace Jovanovich.

————. *Don't You Turn Back—Poetry of Langston Hughes*. Knopf.

————. *Faces and Places: Poems for You*. Scholastic.

————. *Moments: Poems about the Seasons*. Harcourt Brace Jovanovich.

————. *Poetry on Wheels*. Garrard.

————. *Potato Chips and a Slice of Moon*. Scholastic.

————. *Rainbows Are Made*. Harcourt Brace Jovanovich.

————. *To Look at Anything*. Harcourt Brace Jovanovich.

Hughes, Langston. *The Poetry of the Negro, 1746–1970*. Doubleday.

————. *Selected Poems of Langston Hughes*. Random House.

Hughes, Ted. *Moon Whales and Other Poems*. Viking.

————. *Season Songs*. Viking.

————. *Under the North Star*. Viking.

Kennedy, X. J. *The Forgetful Wishing Well*. Atheneum.

Kuskin, Karla. *Dogs, Dragons, Trees and Dreams*. Harper & Row.

————. *Near the Window Tree*. Harper & Row.

————. *A Rose on My Cake*. Harper & Row.

Larrick, Nancy. *Bring Me All Your Dreams*. M. Evans.

————. *More Poetry for Holidays*. Scholastic.

————. *When the Dark Comes Dancing*. Philomel.

Lee, Dennis. *Alligator Pie*. Houghton Mifflin.

Livingston, Myra Cohn. *Celebrations*. Holiday House.

————. *A Circle of Seasons*. Holiday House.

————. *Listen Children Listen*. Harcourt Brace Jovanovich.

————. *Monkey Puzzles*. Atheneum.

————. *O Frabjous Day*. Atheneum.

————. *O Sliver of Liver*. Atheneum.

————. *Sea Songs*. Holiday House.

————. *Sky Songs*. Holiday House.

————. *A Song I Sang to You*. Harcourt Brace Jovanovich.

————. *Why Am I So Cold?*. Atheneum.

Longfellow, Henry Wadsworth. *Hiawatha*. Dutton.

McCord, David. *All Day Long*. Yearling.

————. *Far and Few*. Little, Brown.

————. *One at a Time*. Little, Brown.

McGovern, Ann. *Arrow Book of Poetry*. Scholastic.

Merriam, Eve. *Jamboree: Rhymes for All Times*. Dell.

————. *A Sky Full of Poems*. Dell.

————. *A Word or Two with You*. Atheneum.

Millay, Edna St. Vincent. *Poems–Selected for Young People*. Harper & Row.

Milne, A. A. *Now We Are Six*. Methuen.

————. *When We Were Very Young*. Dell.

Moore, Lilian. *Go with the Poem*. McGraw-Hill.

————. *Think of Shadows*. Atheneum.

————. *To See the World Afresh*. Atheneum.

Nash, Ogden. *The Moon Is Shining Bright as Day*. Lippincott.

O'Neill, Mary. *Fingers Are Always Bringing in the News*. Doubleday.

————. *Hailstones and Halibut Bones*. Doubleday.

————. *What Is That Sound!* Atheneum.

————. *Winds*. Doubleday.

Opie, Iona, and Peter Opie. *The Oxford Book of Narrative Verse*. Oxford.

Prelutsky, Jack. *Circus*. Macmillan.

————. *The Headless Horseman Rides Tonight*. Greenwillow.

————. *It's Snowing! It's Snowing!* Greenwillow.

————. *It's Thanksgiving*. Scholastic.

————. *The New Kid on the Block*. Scholastic.

————. *Nightmares*. Greenwillow.

————. *The Queen of Eene*. Greenwillow.

————. *The Random House Book of Poetry for Children*. Random House.

————. *Read-Aloud Rhymes: For the Very Young*. Knopf.

————. *Zoo Doings*. Greenwillow.

Sandburg, Carl. *Early Moon*. Harcourt Brace Jovanovich.

————. *Rainbows Are Made*. Harcourt Brace Jovanovich.

————. *Wind Song.* Voyager.
Service, Robert W. *Best Tales of the Yukon.* Running Press.
Silverstein, Shel. *The Light in the Attic.* Harper & Row.
————. *Where the Sidewalk Ends.* Harper & Row.
Viorst, Judith. *If I Were in Charge of the World.* Atheneum.
Zolotow, Charlotte. *River Winding.* Crowell.

Recommended Reading

Baldwin, Neil. *The Poetry Writing Handbook*. New York: Scholastic Book Services, 1981.

Brooks, Cleanth, and Robert Penn Warren. *Understanding Poetry*. 4th ed. New York: Holt, Rinehart & Winston, 1976.

Brown, Rosellen, et al., eds. *The Whole Word Catalogue*. New York: Teachers & Writers Collaborative, 1972.

Calkins, Lucy McCormick. *The Art of Teaching Writing*. Portsmouth, N.H.: Heinemann Educational Books, 1986.

Ciardi, John. *How Does a Poem Mean?* Boston: Houghton Mifflin, 1959.

Collom, Jack. *Moving Windows: Evaluating the Poetry Children Write*. New York: Teachers & Writers Collaborative, 1985.

Dunning, Stephen; M. Joe Eaton; and Malcolm Glass. *For Poets*. New York: Scholastic Book Services, 1975.

Grossman, Florence. *Getting from Here to There: Writing and Reading Poetry*. Upper Montclair, N.J.: Boynton Cook, 1982.

Hopkins, Lee Bennett. *Pass the Poetry, Please*. New York: Citation Press, 1972.

Hugo, Richard. *The Triggering Town: Lectures and Essays on Poetry and Writing*. New York: W. W. Norton, 1979.

Kennedy, X. J., and Dorothy M. Kennedy. *Knock at a Star: A Child's Introduction to Poetry*. Boston: Little, Brown, 1982.

Koch, Kenneth. *Rose, Where Did You Get That Red?* New York: Vintage Books, 1973.

———. *Wishes, Lies and Dreams*. New York: Vintage Books, 1970.

Koch, Kenneth, and Kate Farrell. *Sleeping on the Wing*. New York: Vintage Books, 1982.

Lathem, Edward Connery, and Lawrance Thompson, eds. *Robert Frost: Poetry and Prose*. New York: Holt, Rinehart & Winston, 1972.

Livingston, Myra Cohn. *The Child as Poet: Myth or Reality*. Boston: Horn Book, 1984.

Martin, Bill Jr, and Peggy Brogan. *Sounds of Language*. New York: Holt, Rinehart & Winston, 1973.

McKim, Elizabeth, and Judith W. Steinberg. *Beyond Words: Writing Poems with Children*. Green Harbor, Mass.: Wampeter Press, 1983.

Norton, Donna E. *Through the Eyes of a Child*. Columbus, Ohio: Charles E. Merrill, 1983.

Norton, James H., and Frances Gretton. *Writing Incredibly Short Plays, Poems, Stories*. New York: Harcourt Brace Jovanovich, 1972.

Nyhart, Nina, and Kinereth Gensler. *The Poetry Connection*. New York: Teachers and Writers Collaborative, 1978.

Padgett, Ron, ed. *Handbook of Poetic Forms*. New York: Teachers & Writers Collaborative, 1987.

Perrine, Laurence. *Sound and Sense: An Introduction to Poetry*. 3d ed. New York: Harcourt, Brace, & World, 1969.

Raffel, Burton. *How to Read a Poem*. New York: New American Library, 1984.

Smith, Frank. *Reading Without Nonsense*. New York: Teachers College Press, 1985.

Terry Ann. *Children's Poetry Preferences: A National Survey of Upper Elementary Grades*. No. 16 in a series of research reports. Urbana, Ill.: National Council of Teachers of English Committee of Research, 1972.

Turco, Lewis. *Poetry: An Introduction Through Writing*. Reston, Va.: Reston, 1973.

Walter, Nina Willis. *Let Them Write Poetry*. New York: Holt, Rinehart & Winston, 1962.

Zavatsky, Bill, and Ron Padgett, eds. *The Whole Word Catalogue 2*. New York: McGraw Hill in association with Teachers & Writers Collaborative, 1977.

WORKS CITED

Calkins, Lucy McCormick. 1986. *The Art of Teaching Writing.* Portsmouth, N.H.: Heinemann Educational Books.

Ciardi, John. 1958. "Robert Frost: The Way to the Poem." In *Robert Frost: An Introduction*, ed. Robert A. Greenberg and James G. Hepburn. New York: Holt, Rinehart and Winston, 1961.

Collom, Jack. 1985. *Moving Windows: Evaluating the Poetry Children Write.* New York: Teachers & Writers Collaborative.

Gurley, George H. Jr. 1986. "Poets Find the Words We Need" in the column "Behind the Lines." *Kansas City Star* (February 1).

Heath, Shirley Brice. 1983. *Ways with Words: Language, Life and Work in Communities and Classrooms.* Cambridge: Cambridge University Press.

Hill, Helen M. 1979. "How To Tell a Sheep from a Goat—and Why It Matters." *Horn Book Magazine* (February).

Holland, William W. 1982. "The Unseen Worth" from the section "The Home Front." *Christian Science Monitor* (July 22).

Hopkins, Lee Bennett. 1972. *Pass the Poetry, Please.* New York: Citation Press.

Hugo, Richard. 1979. *The Triggering Town: Lectures and Essays on Poetry and Writing.* New York: W. W. Norton.

Koch, Kenneth. 1970. *Wishes, Lies and Dreams.* New York: Random House.

————. 1973. *Rose, Where Did You Get That Red?* New York: Random House.

Koch, Kenneth, and Kate Farrell. 1982. *Sleeping on the Wing.* New York: Random House.

Lathem, Edward C., and Lawrance Thompson. 1972. *Robert Frost, Poetry and Prose.* New York: Holt, Rinehart & Winston.

Livingston, Myra Cohn. 1984. *The Child as Poet: Myth or Reality.* Boston: Horn Book.

Martin, Bill Jr, and Peggy Brogan. 1972. *Teacher's Guide, Sounds Jubilee and Sounds Freedomring.* New York: Holt, Rinehart & Winston, Inc.

———. 1972. *Sounds of a Young Hunter.* New York: Holt, Rinehart & Winston.

Martin, Bill Jr, John Archambault, and Peggy Brogan. 1986. *Treasure Chest of Poetry.* Allen, Texas: Developmental Learning Materials Teaching Resources.

Naisbitt, John. 1982. *Megatrends: Ten New Directions Transforming Our Lives.* New York: Warner Books.

Norton, Donna E. 1983. *Through the Eyes of a Child: An Introduction to Children's Literature.* Columbus, Ohio: Charles E. Merrill.

Sandburg, Carl. 1970. *The Complete Poems of Carl Sandburg.* New York: Harcourt Brace Jovanovich.

Smith, Frank. 1985. *Reading Without Nonsense.* New York: Teacher's College Press.

Taelen, Thomas, et al. 1984. *The Stone Circle Anthology.* Kewadin, Mich.: The Stone Circle Press.

Terry, Ann. 1972. *Children's Poetry Preferences: A National Survey of Upper Elementary Grades.* No. 16 in a series of research reports. Urbana, Ill.: National Council of Teachers of English Committee of Research.

Thomas, Dylan. 1968. "Notes on the Art of Poetry." In *Modern Culture and the Arts,* ed. James B. Hall and Barry Ulanov. New York: McGraw Hill.

Trelease, Jim. 1982. *The Read-Aloud Handbook.* New York: Penguin Books.

ACKNOWLEDGMENTS

(Continued from page iv)

Chapter 2: "Dreams" from *The Dream Keeper and Other Poems* by Langston Hughes. Copyright 1932 by Alfred A. Knopf, Inc. and renewed 1960 by Langston Hughes. Reprinted by permission of Alfred A. Knopf, Inc.

Chapter 2: "Feelings About Words" from *Words Words Words* by Mary O'Neill. Copyright © 1966 by Mary O'Neill. Reprinted by permission of Doubleday Publishing, a division of Bantam, Doubleday, Dell Publishing Group Inc.

Chapter 2: "Little Girl, Be Careful What You Say." From *The Complete Poems of Carl Sandburg*, copyright 1950 by Carl Sandburg; renewed 1978 by Margaret Sandburg, Helga Sandburg Crile and Janet Sandburg. Reprinted by permission of Harcourt Brace Jovanovich, Inc.

Chapters 2 and 5: "Something Told the Wild Geese." Reprinted with permission of Macmillan Publishing Company from *Branches Green* by Rachel Field. Copyright 1934 by Macmillan Publishing Company, renewed 1962 by Arthur S. Pederson.

Chapter 3: "The Pickety Fence." From *One at a Time* by David McCord. Copyright © 1952 by David McCord. Copyright © 1961, 1962 by David McCord. By permission of Little, Brown and Company.

Chapters 3 and 5: "Alligator Pie" by Dennis Lee from *Alligator Pie*, published by Macmillan of Canada, © 1974, Dennis Lee.

Chapter 3: "Where?" From *One at a Time* by David McCord. Copyright © 1952 by David McCord. Copyright © 1961, 1962 by David McCord. By permission of Little, Brown and Company.

Chapter 3: Refrain from *Millions of Cats* by Wanda Gag, copyright

1928 by Coward-McCann, Inc., copyright renewed © 1956 by Robert Janssen. Reprinted by permission of Coward-McCann, Inc.

Chapter 3: "Five Little Bats" by David McCord. From *One at a Time* by David McCord. Copyright © 1952 by David McCord. Copyright © 1961, 1962 by David McCord. By permission of Little, Brown and Company.

Chapter 3: "in Just—" is reprinted from *Tulips & Chimneys* by E. E. Cummings by permission of Liveright Publishing Corporation. Copyright 1923, 1925 and renewed 1951, 1953 by E. E. Cummings. Copyright © 1973, 1976 by the Trustees for the E. E. Cummings Trust. Copyright © 1973, 1976 by George James Firmage.

Chapter 3: "!blac" by E. E. Cummings. Copyright 1940 by E. E. Cummings; renewed 1968 by Marion Morehouse Cummings. Reprinted from *Complete Poems, 1913–1962* by E. E. Cummings by permission of Harcourt Brace Jovanovich, Inc.

Chapter 3: "The Kind of Bath for Me" by Sir Edward Parry. Previously printed in *Sounds of Language* reading series and *Treasure Chest of Poetry*. Used by permission of Bill Martin Jr.

Chapters 3 and 5: "Birches" from *The Poetry of Robert Frost* edited by Edward Connery Lathem. Copyright © 1969 by Holt, Rinehart and Winston, Inc. Copyright © 1962 by Robert Frost. Copyright © 1975 by Lesley Frost Ballantine. Reprinted by permission of Henry Holt and Company, Inc.

Chapter 3: From "Staying Alive" by David Wagoner in *David Wagoner: Collected Poems, 1956–1976*; published by Indiana University Press, 1976. Copyright © David Wagoner. Reprinted by permission.

Chapter 5: "Unfolding Bud" by Naoshi Koriyama. Reprinted by permission from *The Christian Science Monitor*. © 1957 The Christian Science Publishing Society. All rights reserved.

Chapter 5: "Poem" by Langston Hughes. From *The Dream Keeper and Other Poems* by Langston Hughes. Copyright 1932 by Alfred A. Knopf, Inc. and renewed 1960 by Langston Hughes. Reprinted by permission of Alfred A. Knopf, Inc.

Chapter 6: "On A Snowy Day" by Dorothy Aldis reprinted by permission of G.P. Putnam's Sons from *All Together* by Dorothy Aldis, copyright 1925–1928, 1934, 1939, 1952, copyright renewed © 1953–1956, 1962, 1967 by Dorothy Aldis.

Chapter 6: "Ice Cream" by John Archambault. From *DLM's Treasure Chest of Poetry*. Copyright © 1986 by Developmental Learning Materials (DLM). Reprinted by permission of John Archambault.

Chapter 6: "Cat" by Mary Britton Miller. Copyright estate of Mary Britton Miller. Reprinted by permission.

INDEX OF POEMS AND POETS